Carolyn Barraclough
and Suzanne Gaynor

Student's BOOK

B1

Keep it REAL!

Contents

	LANGUAGE		**SKILLS**	
	VOCABULARY	**GRAMMAR**	**READING**	**LISTENING**
Starter unit p4	› Hobbies and interests	› Adjectives › Irregular past simple verbs › Present continuous and present simple		
Unit 1 Unforgettable p9	› -ed and -ing adjectives › Vlog › Arts and entertainment	› used to › Pronunciation: used to /juːst tə/ › Past simple vs past continuous › Grammar animations	› Remember that? › Skill: Understanding the main idea of a text › Word Power: Antonyms	› Carnival time › Skill: Identifying specific information in a podcast
Unit 2 Time to go! p19	› Verbs for travel and holidays › Vlog › Nouns for travel	› Present perfect with ever/never, been/gone › Present perfect with just, already, yet › Pronunciation: have/has: strong and weak forms › Grammar animations	› Picture perfect › Skill: Finding specific detail in a blog post › Word Power: Place names	› Has the train left? › Skill: Identifying key information in announcements
Unit 3 Eat up! p29	› Food and drink adjectives › Vlog › Cooking methods and menus	› Present perfect with How long...?, for and since › Present perfect and past simple › Pronunciation: /s/, /z/ and /ɪz/ › Grammar animations	› Silent snacks › Skill: Using pictures for prediction › Word Power: Verbs of the senses	› That's unusual! › Skill: Identifying specific information in an interview
REVIEW UNITS 1–3 pp100–101			**PROJECTS UNITS 1–3 pp106–107**	
Unit 4 Dream big p39	› Jobs and job sectors › Vlog › Adjectives of personality	› Future forms › Pronunciation: 'll › First conditional: if and unless/ might vs will + adverbs › Grammar animations	› What happens when ...? › Skill: Understanding pronoun references › Word Power: Social media nouns and verbs	› Right for the job › Skill: Identifying personal information in a podcast
Unit 5 Get the message? p49	› Communication verbs › Vlog › Communication nouns	› Second conditional › Obligation, necessity and advice: need to/must/have to; should/ought to › Grammar animations	› How we communicate › Skill: Understanding details in a report › Word Power: physical and spoken forms of communication	› Express yourself › Skill: Identifying opinions › Pronunciation: Emphasis
Unit 6 Teamwork p59	› Sports actions and events › Vlog › Adverbs of manner	› Relative pronouns; Indefinite pronouns › Pronunciation: Emphasis › Ability and permission: can, could, be able to; be allowed to › Grammar animations	› Bringing a magical sport to life › Skill: Working out the meaning of unknown words › Word Power: Phrasal verbs	› Team building › Skill: Understanding the main points that different speakers make
REVIEW UNITS 4–6 pp102–103			**PROJECTS UNITS 4–6 pp108–109**	
Unit 7 Rainbow Earth p69	› The natural environment › Vlog › Environment verbs	› Present simple passive › Past simple passive › Pronunciation: Weak forms /wəz/ /wə/ or strong forms /wɒz/ /wɜː/ › Grammar animations	› Nature in brilliant blue! › Skill: Scanning texts to find a main idea › Word Power: Words connected to animals and plants	› It's important ... › Skill: Using questions to predict what information to listen for
Unit 8 The learning zone p79	› Education words › Vlog › Phrasal verbs	› Past perfect simple › Modals of possibility and certainty › Pronunciation: Sentence stress › Grammar animations	› A warm welcome › Skill: Using titles and headings to make predictions › Word Power: Words related to snow, winter and cold weather	› It could be fun! › Skill: Recognizing a speaker's attitude and feelings
Unit 9 Your choice p89	› Shopping nouns › Vlog › Adjectives and affixes	› Reported speech › Reported questions › Grammar animations	› The Teenage Market › Skill: Scanning for specific information › Word Power: Phrasal verbs	› Do the right thing › Skill: Taking notes about the order of events
REVIEW UNITS 7–9 pp104–105			**PROJECTS UNITS 7–9 pp110–111**	
REFERENCE	**EXAM PRACTICE UNITS 1–9 pp118–126**		**LANGUAGE SUMMARY UNITS 1–9 pp127–135**	

SPEAKING	WRITING	CULTURE	21ST CENTURY SKILLS
› Comparative and superlative adjectives	› Past simple	› Quantifiers: *some, any, (how) much, (how) many, a lot of*	
› *What's on...?* › **Skill:** Asking and answering questions about past events › **Useful language:** Asking and answering questions › 👁 *Keep moving!*	› *A story* › **Skill:** Writing about a special event in the past › **Useful language:** Time phrases › **Look!** Connectors	› *A museum with a difference* › **Word Power:** Verb and noun collocations › 👁 **Culture video**	🔍 **FIND OUT** p17 💬 **THINK CRITICALLY** p10 🌐 **COMPARE CULTURES** p17 💡 **GET CREATIVE** p14
› *Can you help us?* › **Skill:** Asking for help and information › **Useful language:** Asking for help; Giving information › 👁 *Keep moving!*	› *An email* › **Skill:** Writing about my holiday news › **Useful language:** Writing about past events › **Look!** *really, so, such*	› *Something to take home* › **Word Power:** Compound nouns › 👁 **Culture video**	🔍 **FIND OUT** p19 💬 **THINK CRITICALLY** p27 🌐 **COMPARE CULTURES** p21 💡 **GET CREATIVE** p27
› *I'd prefer pizza* › **Skill:** Expressing preferences › **Useful language:** Expressing present and future preferences › 👁 *Keep moving!*	› *A description* › **Skill:** Writing a description of a special meal › **Useful language:** Describing a meal › **Look!** Order of adjectives	› *International flavour* › **Word Power:** Places where you can buy meals › 👁 **Culture video**	🔍 **FIND OUT** p31 💬 **THINK CRITICALLY** p30 🌐 **COMPARE CULTURES** p29 💡 **GET CREATIVE** p37

LITERATURE UNITS 1–3 pp.112–113

› *What next?* › **Skill:** Giving reasons to support my point of view › **Useful language:** Giving opinions › 👁 *Keep moving!*	› *A letter* › **Skill:** Writing a letter about my future plans › **Useful language:** Speculating about the future › **Look!** Future time expressions	› *Top teenage jobs* › **Word Power:** Word families › 👁 **Culture video**	🔍 **FIND OUT** p42 💬 **THINK CRITICALLY** p47 🌐 **COMPARE CULTURES** p47 💡 **GET CREATIVE** p40
› *Do you really mean that?* › **Skill:** Asking for and giving clarification › **Useful language:** Giving and asking for clarification › 👁 *Keep moving!*	› *Advice forum* › **Skill:** Writing advice in a forum › **Useful language:** Giving reasons › **Look!** Talking about purpose	› *Not the only language* › **Word Power:** Language nouns › 👁 **Culture video**	🔍 **FIND OUT** p50 💬 **THINK CRITICALLY** p57 🌐 **COMPARE CULTURES** p57 💡 **GET CREATIVE** p54
› *Have a go!* › **Skill:** Preparing a group presentation › **Useful language:** Giving a group presentation › 👁 *Keep moving!*	› *FAQs* › **Skill:** Writing clear and useful information › **Useful language:** Using questions as headings › **Look!** Making adjectives stronger or weaker	› *Who do you support?* › **Word Power:** Sports places, people and equipment › 👁 **Culture video**	🔍 **FIND OUT** p67 💬 **THINK CRITICALLY** p67 🌐 **COMPARE CULTURES** p64 💡 **GET CREATIVE** p60

LITERATURE UNITS 4–6 pp.114–115

› *Plastic free!* › **Skill:** Agreeing and disagreeing › **Useful language:** Agreeing and disagreeing › 👁 *Keep moving!*	› *A for and against essay* › **Skill:** Writing an essay about the environment › **Useful language:** Arguing for and against › **Look!** Giving more information	› *Animal protection* › **Word Power:** Nouns related to verbs › 👁 **Culture video**	🔍 **FIND OUT** p69 💬 **THINK CRITICALLY** p77 🌐 **COMPARE CULTURES** p77 💡 **GET CREATIVE** p70
› *Did you hear about ...?* › **Skill:** Asking for news and reacting › **Useful language:** Asking for news; Giving news; Reacting › 👁 *Keep moving!*	› *A blog post* › **Skill:** Writing an informal blog post › **Useful language:** Using informal language › **Look!** Exclamatory phrases	› *Learning together* › **Word Power:** Words and expressions related to time and periods of life › 👁 **Culture video**	🔍 **FIND OUT** p87 🌐 **COMPARE CULTURES** p80 💬 **THINK CRITICALLY** p82 💡 **GET CREATIVE** p87
› *You won't regret it!* › **Skill:** Persuading › **Pronunciation:** Intonation › **Useful language:** Being persuasive › 👁 *Keep moving!*	› *A review* › **Skill:** Writing a review of a shop or a website › **Useful language:** Writing a review › **Look!** Recommending	› *Shopping adventure* › **Word Power:** Compound nouns › 👁 **Culture video**	🔍 **FIND OUT** p97 💬 **THINK CRITICALLY** p89 🌐 **COMPARE CULTURES** p97 💡 **GET CREATIVE** p90

LITERATURE UNITS 7–9 pp116–117

IRREGULAR VERBS LIST ppp136

Starter

VOCABULARY Hobbies and interests

I can talk about hobbies and interests.

1 🔊 S0.1 Match the expressions with the pictures. Listen and check.

> chat with friends   do exercise   go for a walk
> go shopping   make a vlog   make cakes
> play an instrument   play computer games
> take photos   watch films

2 Copy the headings. Make lists with the expressions in Exercise 1. Add more activities to each list.

> Activities you usually do at home

> Activities you do usually do somewhere else

> Activities you usually do alone

> Activities you usually do with friends

3 Work in pairs. Discuss the activities. When and where do you do them?

A: I usually go shopping in the shopping centre on Saturdays. What about you?
B: I don't go shopping often. It's boring!

Adjectives

I can use common adjectives.

4 🔊 S0.2 Complete the article with the adjectives in the box. Listen and check.

> beautiful   clever   cool   difficult   easy
> fun   funny   interesting   nice   scary

The bloggers ...

I'm Beth and I enjoy making cakes with my friend Levi. We put recipes on our blog and people write a lot of ¹… comments. I write the blog and Levi takes the photos. It isn't ²… to get good photos of food, but Levi's photos are always ³… . Cooking isn't our only hobby – we love watching films, too. Levi likes ⁴… films with zombies, but I prefer ⁵… films! We're thinking of starting a blog about our favourite films. If you think this idea for a blog is ⁶…, let us know!

and the vlogger

Hi, I'm Alfie, and I'm a vlogger. There are lots of fashion vlogs for girls, but there aren't many for boys. I want to change that, so I make videos about ⁷… new styles and clothes. I make my vlog when I go shopping and when I'm at home. I love making my vlog – it's really ⁸… . But it's ⁹… to edit the videos, so my brother helps me. He's really ¹⁰… with computers.

5 Read the article again. Who does these things? Write *Beth*, *Levi* or *Alfie*.

Who …
  enjoys making cakes? *Beth*
1 enjoys taking photos?
2 enjoys making videos?
3 loves watching films?
4 has plans for a new project?
5 has help from a family member?

> **Look!** *fun* and *funny*
>
> *fun* and *funny* are both adjectives.
> Compare the sentences:
> We do **fun** activities at the weekend. (I enjoy them.)
> Jacob is very **funny**. (I laugh when I'm with him.)

GRAMMAR
Present continuous and present simple

I can use the present simple and present continuous.

1 Read the grammar box. Copy and complete the rules with the words in the box.

> habits and repeated actions
> things that are happening now or around now

	Present simple	Present continuous
+	My brother **helps** me with my vlog.	We**'re thinking** of starting a blog about films.
–	I **don't like** scary films.	Levi **isn't taking** a photo right now.
?	**Do** you **read** our blog?	What **are** you **doing** today?

Rules

We use the present simple for [1] ... . We often use it with time expressions like *sometimes, every day*, etc.

We use the present continuous for [2] ... . We often use time expressions like *at the moment, right now, today*.

2 Rewrite the sentences using the negative form.

> Nathan goes camping every year.
> *Nathan doesn't go camping every year.*

1 My friends and I are hanging out in the park.
2 They're playing computer games.
3 I write in my diary every evening.
4 Ana meets her friend every day.
5 The teacher is talking to Ahmed.

3 Put the words in the correct order to make questions.

> do / go / what time / to school / you / ?
> *What time do you go to school?*

1 at the weekend / you / see / do / your friends / ?
2 are / what / you / today / in English / studying / ?
3 doing / is / your best friend / what / right now / ?
4 what / after school / do / you and your friends / usually / do / ?
5 enjoying / are / this lesson / you / ?

4 Work in pairs. Ask and answer the questions in Exercise 3. Give extra information.

> What time do you go to school?
>> I leave home at about 7.30 and I arrive at school at 8.05. What about you?

Comparative and superlative adjectives

I can use comparative and superlative adjectives.

5 Copy and complete the grammar box with the correct comparative or superlative form of the adjectives.

	Adjective	Comparative	Superlative
Short adjectives	tall nice big easy	tall**er** [1] ... big**ger** [4] ...	**the** tall**est** [2] ... [3] ... **the** eas**iest**
Long adjectives	difficult interesting	more difficult [6] ...	[5] ... **the most** interesting
Irregular adjectives	good bad	better [8] ...	[7] ... **the worst**

6 Complete the sentences. Use the correct form of the adjective in the box.

> beautiful   difficult   funny   healthy   nice

1 Camping in summer is ... than camping in winter.
2 I think the castle is ... building in our city.
3 Learning the piano is ... than learning the guitar.
4 Fruit salad is ... dessert on this menu.
5 Your jokes are always ... than mine!

7 Complete the text with the correct forms of the verbs and adjectives in brackets.

ASHIMA SHIRAISHI is already one of the [1] ... (good) climbers in the world. Although Ashima was born in New York, her parents [2] ... (come) from Japan. They [3] ... (live) in Tokyo at the moment. Ashima [4] ... (prepare) for the next Olympics. Ashima is [5] ... (small) than some other climbers, but she is [6] ... (strong) than them! She [7] ... (not have) much free time, but she [8] ... (enjoy) going shopping for second-hand clothes. Her mum makes some of her climbing clothes – she [9] ... (wear) some in the photo!

» FAST FINISHER

Write about each of these categories: food, sports, school lessons, films and famous people. Use comparative and superlative adjectives.

Fruit is healthier than cake.
Football is the best sport!

VOCABULARY Irregular past simple verbs

I can make the past simple form of irregular verbs.

1 🔊 S0.3 Read and listen to the school newsletter and match the verbs in the box with the blue past simple forms.

buy	find out	go	have	hear	make	meet	know
put	see	send	take	tell	think	wake up	write

Before 2000

HINKSEY HIGH SCHOOL

Class 10B [1] **went** on a history trip to a hands-on exhibition of technology from the 1980s and 1990s. We [2] **knew** that old technology was very different, but some of the gadgets that we [3] **saw** were crazy! We [4] **found out** a lot about daily life in the past.

1 Our parents [5] **woke up** when they [6] **heard** this every morning.  alarm clock

5 My parents often [13] **met** their friends at the arcades to play these exciting new games.  video games

2 Kids often [7] **took** photos with this. It was quick and very cool. They [8] **put** their photos in an album.  Polaroid camera

6 Teenagers listened to music on this. They [14] **thought** it was really cool.  cassette player

3 People [9] **made** films of family life with this. My mum [10] **told** me it was my grandad's favourite hobby! camcorder

7 Every home [15] **had** this because most people didn't have mobile phones until the late 1990s. landline

4 People often [11] **wrote** and [12] **sent** messages like this. How slow!  letters

8 Families watched films on these. They [16] **bought** them or rented them from a shop or a library. video cassettes

2 Work in pairs. What do you use now instead of the objects in the pictures?

I don't use an alarm clock. I use my phone.

3 Complete each sentence with a past tense verb from Exercise 1.
1. My mum … letters when she was young.
2. We … some great songs from the 1990s.
3. I … some old video cassettes in the attic.
4. Dad's hobby was dancing, so he … a cassette player everywhere!
5. We … to the beach every day when we were on holiday.
6. I … really early this morning because there was a lot of noise outside.
7. I … my aunt's photo albums. Everybody looked so young!
8. My friend … new trainers on Saturday. They look really cool.

4 PRONUNCIATION Different vowel sounds

🔊 S0.4 Listen and repeat the verbs. Pay attention to the different vowel sounds.

h<u>ea</u>r – h<u>ea</u>rd   f<u>ou</u>nd – th<u>ou</u>ght
h<u>a</u>d – m<u>a</u>de   f<u>i</u>nd – l<u>i</u>stened

5 Complete the sentences so that they are true for you.
1. I woke up at … this morning.
2. I saw … on my way to school today.
3. I heard a great song by … last week.
4. I met … at the weekend.
5. Last time I went on holiday, I took … .
6. I had a … when I was younger, but I haven't got it now.

6 Work in groups. Compare your sentences in Exercise 5. Did you have the same answers as another student?

Lara and I both woke up at 6.30 this morning.
David and I both met our cousins at the weekend.

GRAMMAR Past simple

I can use the past simple to talk about past events.

1 Read the grammar box. Copy and complete the rules with the correct words from the box.

affirmative   negative   questions   regular

+	My dad **had** a lot of games like this. Teenagers **listened to** their music on this.
–	I **didn't see** that alien. They **didn't like** it.
?	**Did** people **want** to hear the alarm clock? Yes, they **did**. / No, they **didn't**.

Rules
We use the past simple form in [1] ... sentences. [2] ... verbs end in -ed.
We use didn't + infinitive in [3] ... sentences.
We form [4] ... with did + subject + infinitive.

2 Choose the correct form of the verbs.
1. I didn't *send / sent* any text messages yesterday.
2. Did you *watch / watched* the football last night?
3. Last week, my friends and I *see / saw* a movie.
4. My brother *buy / bought* some new earphones.
5. The teacher didn't *write / wrote* any comments on my homework.

3 Complete the blog post with the correct form of the verbs in brackets.

We [1] ... (find) a lot of old photos at my grandparents' house. Gran [2] ... (not know) what to do with them. She [3] ... (not want) to put them in frames. Then I [4] ... (have) a great idea. I used an app to make a digital photo collage. I [5] ... (make) copies of Gran's photos and added some songs that she likes. I [6] ... (not tell) Gran – I gave her the collage as a birthday surprise. She was so happy when she saw the photos and [7] ... (hear) the songs on my laptop – she [8] ... (love) it!

4 Ask questions to find out three things that your partner did at the weekend. You can only answer *Yes, I did* or *No, I didn't*.

A: *Did you go to the cinema?*
B: *No, I didn't.*

Quantifiers: *some, any, (how) much, (how) many, a lot of*

I can use quantifiers with countable and uncountable nouns.

5 Read the grammar box. Do we use the quantifiers in the box with countable nouns, uncountable nouns, or both?

a lot of   much   many

	Countable	Uncountable
+	You've got **some** / **a lot of** great songs on this cassette.	You've got **some** / **a lot of** great music on this cassette.
–	There aren't **any** / **many** / **a lot of** apps on my phone.	There isn't **any** / **much** / **a lot of** time.
?	Are there **any** / **many** / **a lot of** instructions? **How many** video games have you got?	Is there **any** / **much** / **a lot of** information? **How much** music is there on this cassette?

6 Find the quantifier which we <u>can't</u> use in each sentence.

I've got *much / some / a lot of* free time today.
I've got ~~much~~ / *some / a lot of free time today.*
1. I haven't got *much / some / a lot of* money in my school bag.
2. Have you got *a lot of / many / any* paper? I left my notepad at home.
3. We can't see *any / some / many* people outside.
4. There are *any / a lot of / some* students in the park.
5. Is there *much / many / a lot of* food in the fridge?

7 Complete each question with a quantifier. Sometimes there is more than one possibility.
1. How ... time do you spend on your phone every day?
2. Are there ... good apps on your phone?
3. Have you got ... videos and photos on it?
4. How ... music is on your phone?
5. How ... headphones or earphones do you own?

8 Ask and answer the questions in Exercise 7. Give extra information.

A: *How much time do you spend on your phone every day?*
B: *I think I spend about two hours on it.*

⏩ FAST FINISHER

Write five sentences about your phone. What do you have on it? What do you use it for?
I take a lot of photos on my phone, but I don't have much music on it.

READING

I can find information in a text and answer questions.

1 🔊 **S0.5** Read and listen to the advert and descriptions. Which category do Carla and Emin choose for their photos?

Photography competition

Send us your best photo and tell us why you like it.

Choose a category:

| hobbies | your town | family and friends |

First prize: a three-day photography course

Carla Vidal

I love taking photos, and I've got a really good camera on my phone.

I took this photo of my friend Alex's grandparents. It was their fiftieth wedding anniversary, and they had a big party. She made a cake for her grandparents. In the photo, they're blowing out the candles and everybody is clapping. I like the photo because it's natural – they're really happy, and I like the bright colours. I think it's one of my best photos.

Emin Yilmaz

I recently found an old camera – it was my grandad's. It takes black and white photos, and I think they are really beautiful. This one is my favourite. It's a photo of my sisters, Ela and Melisa. Ela is younger than Melisa, but they love spending time together. They go for walks and watch films. This one is the most interesting photo because they didn't see me. They're in their own little world – just relaxing on the sofa together.

2 Read the texts again. Answer the questions.
1 Why does Carla take photos with her phone?
2 What special occasion was it when Carla took her photo?
3 Why does she think it's a good photo?
4 What is special about the camera that Emin used?
5 What do Ela and Melisa enjoy doing?
6 Why does Emin think it's an interesting photo?

SPEAKING Describing a photo

I can describe a photo in detail.

a

b

3 Look at photos a and b. Which one did Carla take? Which one did Emin take?

4 🔊 **S0.6** Listen to a student describing a photo. Is he describing photo a or b?

5 🔊 **S0.7** Listen and repeat the **Useful language**.

Useful language
Describing a photo
This photo shows …
I think it's … because …
Lots of people are *-ing* …
Everybody is … *-ing*
I'm not sure, but maybe …
I see some / a … at the top / at the bottom / in the middle.

6 Find a photo that you like that includes some people. Make a list of things you can see in the photo using the phrases in the box.

| at the top / bottom | in the background / middle |

7 Work in pairs. Take turns to describe your photo to your partner. Try to talk for about one minute.

» **FAST FINISHER**

Write an entry for the photography competition about a photo that you have taken.

Unforgettable

Vocabulary: -ed and -ing adjectives; Arts and entertainment | **Grammar:** used to...; Past simple vs past continuous | **Speaking:** Talking about a past event | **Writing:** A story

VOCABULARY -ed and -ing adjectives

I can use adjectives ending in -ed and -ing.

1 Work in pairs. Look at the pictures a–c. Where are the people and what are they doing? Match the pictures to the hashtags (#) 1–3.

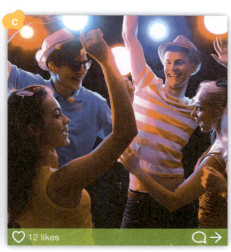

1 #favouritesong #neveragain #embarrassingdad

2 #thebestparty #fun #amazingnight

3 #backtoschool #newfriends #soexciting

2 🔊 1.1 Look at the adjectives in lists A and B. Which list describes a feeling and which describes something that causes a feeling? Listen and check.

A
amazed   amused   annoyed   bored
confused   disappointed   embarrassed
excited   frightened   interested   relaxed
surprised   tired

B
amazing   amusing   annoying   boring
confusing   disappointing   embarrassing
exciting   frightening   interesting
relaxing   surprising   tiring

3 Complete the sentences with the correct -ed or -ing adjectives from Exercise 2.

Jack felt *disappointed* when Mark forgot his birthday.
1 My brother was f... of the lions at the zoo.
2 She never listens to me when I talk. It's very a... .
3 We were s... when my aunt suddenly visited us.
4 The film was very c... , so we didn't understand it.
5 It was a t... day. We left early and got home late.
6 The book was very i... . I read every chapter.
7 I got b... when I listened to the same song every day.
8 We were a... by the comedy show on TV.

Look! **Adjectives from verbs**

We form some adjectives from verbs.
amaze – amazed/amazing
annoy – annoyed/annoying
bore – bored/boring

4 Work in pairs. Complete the questions with the correct form of the word in brackets. Ask and answer the questions.

1 Are you ... (frighten) by horror films?
2 Is learning English more ... (tire) for you than Maths?
3 What sport do you think is ... (excite) to watch?
4 What is an ... (amaze) place to visit in your country?
5 What hobby is ... (relax) for you?

5 With your partner, discuss the questions.

1 When did you last feel disappointed/frightened/surprised?
2 What situations do you think are amusing/annoying/relaxing?

Now watch the vlog.

» FAST FINISHER

Complete the sentence in as many ways as you can.
It's ... when ... .
It's exciting when your team wins a football match.

LS Language summary: Unit 1 **SB** p. 127

Remember that?

READING

I can understand and identify the main idea of a text.

1 Look at the pictures and the words in the box. What type of memories do the pictures show?

family   friends   hobbies   pets   school life

2 🔊 1.2 Read and listen to the posts. What is the main idea of each post?

Teenvibe — SHARE THE MEMORIES
Our heads are full of amazing memories. Here are some of your stories.

NAOMI, 16

I was worried about my first day at my new school. I used to be shy, and I was nervous because there were lots of people I didn't know. My first day was better than I expected. Everybody was friendly, and my classes were interesting. I also met Mac. He was really relaxed and chilled. We're best friends now. He tells terrible jokes and he can be annoying, but he's never boring and thanks to him, I'm no longer shy.

My brother Krish and I used to share a bedroom. Did we use to argue? Yes, we did! I was older and tidy; he was younger and very messy. He didn't use to put anything away. One day, I tripped over his dirty football boots. There was mud all over the carpet. I got some tape and made a line across the floor. He was annoyed, but he kept his things on his side of the room. Eventually, I got my own room. It's clean, but I miss sharing with him.

ANIK, 16

JORDI, 15

I was very excited when I got my dog, Tucker. He used to sleep a lot when he was little, but he was also very active. He used to jump up and down and run around the house in the evening. Once, when he was doing this, there was a loud bang in the living room. When we entered the room, we found the TV on the floor. My parents were really annoyed. I had to take Tucker to training classes after that. We used to go every week, and now he's the perfect pet!

3 🔊 1.2 Read and listen again. Are the sentences true (T) or false (F)? Correct the false sentences.
1. Naomi was excited about her first day at school.
2. Naomi's first day was disappointing.
3. Anik and his brother were quite different.
4. Anik's brother liked the tape across the floor.
5. Tucker was energetic in the evening.
6. Jordi's mother taught the dog how to behave.

4 **Word Power** Find pairs of words with opposite meanings in the text.

older / younger, ...

FUN FACT The nerves we use to detect smells enter the brain in the area responsible for emotions and memories. That's why smells often trigger memories.

5 💬 **THINK CRITICALLY** In pairs, answer the questions.

What brings back memories for you: a smell, a sound or a picture? What is your earliest memory?

GRAMMAR *used to*

I can use *used to* to talk about past habits and routines.

👁 Now watch the grammar animation.

1 Read the rules. Copy and complete the grammar box.

| did (x3) | didn't | didn't use to | use (x2) | used to |

Affirmative	Negative
I **used to** be shy.	He [2] ... put anything away.
He [1] ... sleep a lot.	
Questions	**Short answers**
[3] ... he [4] ... **to** tidy his room?	Yes, he **did**. / No, he [5] ... .
[6] ... we [7] ... **to** argue?	Yes, we [8] ... . / No, we **didn't**.

Rules

We use *used to* to talk about past habits and old routines. We use *used to* when the state or action doesn't happen now.

We use the infinitive *use* (not *used*) in negative sentences and questions.

2 🔊 1.3 Complete the dialogue with the affirmative, negative or question form of *used to*. Listen and check.

Laura: Is that a photo of you? That's so cute!
Abel: Yes, it was my birthday. I used to love parties.
Laura: That's a great costume. [1] ... dress up a lot?
Abel: All the time. That was my favourite costume. It's Yoda from *Star Wars*.
Laura: I know. I [2] ... have one just like it!
Abel: Have you got any photos of you in it?
Laura: Probably, but not at my birthday parties.
Abel: Why's that?
Laura: I [3] ... have parties. My birthday's in August, so it's always during the school holidays.

3 Complete the sentences with the correct form of *used to* and the verb in brackets.

1 I ... (go) to bed at seven o'clock when I was five.
2 '... (you / watch) cartoons after school?' 'Yes, I ... .'
3 My brother ... (not like) basketball, but now he plays every day.
4 '... (Ben / play) in a band?' 'No, he ... .'
5 My best friend and I ... (be) in the same class, but now we aren't.
6 Jane ... (love) eating chocolate, but now she hates it.

4 Complete the facts with the correct form of *used to* and the verbs in the box.

| drink | have | not wash | not sleep | take | ~~write~~ |

Intelligent and creative, but these famous people had some unusual habits!

The English writer Jane Austen worked completely alone. She *used to write* in a room with a noisy door so she knew when someone was coming in.

Leonardo da Vinci loved sleeping, but he [1] ... during the night. He slept 15–20 minutes every four hours. That means he [2] ... about two hours sleep in total.

The historian and writer Voltaire [3] ... between 40 and 50 cups of coffee every day. He lived until he was 83!

Beethoven [4] ... very often and his clothes were dirty. His friends [5] ... his clothes away and wash them when he was asleep!

5 PRONUNCIATION *used to* /juːst tə/

🔊 1.4 Listen and repeat.

1 They used to live in a flat.
2 We used to meet in the park.
3 He used to go out a lot.
4 I used to love rock music.

6 Work in pairs. Write questions with *used to* using the verbs in the box. Ask and answer the questions.

| collect | dress up | drink | eat | go |
| like | make | play | sleep | watch |

A: Did you use to watch cartoons?
B: No, I didn't, but I used to watch ...

» FAST FINISHER

Think about someone in your family. Write three sentences using *used to*.

LS Language summary: Unit 1 **SB** p. 127

Carnival time

VOCABULARY and LISTENING Arts and entertainment

I can identify specific information in a podcast.

1 Look at the pictures and headings. What are the articles about? Read the texts and check your answers.

2 Study the blue nouns. How do you say these words in your language?

WHAT'S ON THIS WEEKEND?
This Week's Events

What a performer Sat 5th
Tracy Dale comes from a family of entertainers. She used to be an acrobat and her grandfather worked in a travelling fair! Tracy owns *The Circus Workshop*. She teaches people to juggle, walk on stilts, do acrobatics and more!

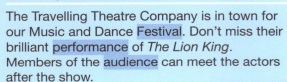

Great entertainment! Sun 6th
The Travelling Theatre Company is in town for our Music and Dance Festival. Don't miss their brilliant performance of *The Lion King*. Members of the audience can meet the actors after the show.

All the way from Brazil Sun 6th
The Rio Carnival is famous around the world for the amazing costumes that people wear in the parade.

See them for yourselves at a new photography exhibition of carnival costumes from Rio. Our reporter says the photos are amazing!

3 🔊 1.5 Copy and complete the table with the blue words from the text. Listen and check.

outdoor events	people	other nouns
festival	audience	entertainment

4 Read the introduction to a local news podcast. Why was everybody looking at Zara?

Colourful carnival

Our photographer, Dan, took some great shots of people while they were walking in the carnival parade. Everybody noticed Zara West on her tall stilts. The youth club members were also popular with the audience. When our photographer met them, they were juggling in their bright circus costumes to raise money for a new youth club centre.

In this podcast, we share memories of a great parade! **LISTEN now**

5 🔊 1.6 Listen to the carnival podcast. How was each person feeling when the parade started?

6 🔊 1.6 Listen again and choose the correct answers.
1 How tall was Zara on her stilts?
   a 1.5 metres   b 2.5 metres   c 2.3 metres
2 How was Ash feeling at the end of the parade?
   a excited   b tired   c embarrassed
3 How much money was in Hugo's bucket?
   a £50   b £100   c £200
4 What was Leo doing when the parade started?
   a barking   b running   c jumping

LS Language summary: Unit 1 SB p. 127

GRAMMAR Past simple vs past continuous

I can use the past simple and past continuous to talk about past events.

👁 Now watch the grammar animation.

1 Read the grammar box. Copy the rules and choose the correct word to complete them.

Past simple	Past continuous
Dan **took** photos **while** they **were walking** in the parade.	
Past continuous	Past simple
We **were walking** in the parade **when** Dan **took** photos of us.	

Rules

We often use the past continuous and the past simple tenses in the same sentence.

We use the [1] *past simple / past continuous* to describe the completed action.

We use the [2] *past simple / past continuous* to describe the action that was in progress.

We use [3] *when / while* before the past simple.

We use [4] *when / while* before the past continuous.

2 Look at the sentences and decide which action was in progress (1) and which was completed (2).

We were watching **(1)** the parade when we saw **(2)** our teacher.
1 While I was talking to the reporter, my phone rang.
2 Ash was riding a bike when it started to snow.
3 We took photos while the band was playing.
4 It was still raining when a rainbow appeared.
5 When Maya took this selfie, she was having fun at the fair.

3 Work in pairs. Use the table to make four sentences with *when* or *while*.

(while)	I was eating a burger	(when)	my friend took a photo
	we were waiting for the teacher		a bird flew into the room
	we were having a test		I dropped my phone
	our teacher was talking		my friend texted me

While I was eating a burger, I dropped my phone.
I was eating a burger when I dropped my phone.

4 🔊 1.7 Write the correct form of the verbs in brackets to complete the text. Listen and check.

LATEST NEWS Local Global

Office workers [1] … (have) a meeting in Minnesota, in the USA, when a racoon [2] … (climb) past their window. Why were they surprised? The office was on the twenty-second floor! The racoon was interesting entertainment, but they were worried for its safety. The racoon was feeling tired and hungry, so it [3] … (rest) for a while, but then it climbed even higher. When it [4] … (reach) the top, a rescue team [5] … (wait) for it.

In a carnival parade in Melbourne, Australia, Tania Makri [6] … (ride) a pony when it ran into the crowd. Tania said, 'Silver usually loves an audience, but she was frightened by some dogs! At the time, I [7] … (not look) at the crowd, so I [8] … (not see) the dogs. Luckily, everybody was OK.'

5 Work in pairs. Make questions using the table below. Ask and answer the questions.

A: What were you doing at 8.00 this morning?
B: I was looking for my homework.

What was/were	you your friend you and your friends	doing when	the school bell rang? your teacher came into the classroom?
		doing at	9.00 yesterday evening? 8.00 this morning? 2 p.m. last Saturday?

» **FAST FINISHER**

Think about an unusual event you saw. What were you doing at the time? Write three sentences with *when* or *while*.

LS Language summary: Unit 1 SB p. 127

What's on ...?
READING and LISTENING

 identify important information in adverts.

 Profile | Home

What's on this autumn?

a Bloxford Skatepark

Sunday 10 October — 10 a.m. – 12 p.m. Ages 10–14
1–4 p.m. – Ages 15–18

Join us to learn about graffiti art!
- All paint provided.
- Beware – it gets messy. Bring old clothes to paint in!
- Certificates for all who attend the event.

Tickets: £5 per person (includes a snack)

20 interested ▼

b Bloxford Town Hall

Saturday 16 October — Open until 11 p.m.

Photography competition
- This year's theme is 'Friends'. Free photography course for the winner!

Live entertainment
- Performances from local bands from 6 p.m.
- Handmade jewellery and gifts.
- Food and drink on sale all day.

Fairground rides in the town square: £3 per ride

45 Going ▼

c Sports Hall

Sunday 24 October — 2–7 p.m.

Calling all students aged 15+!
Learn to be happy, positive and calm.
- Loose clothing only, please.
- Free yoga class at 7.30 for all workshop participants.
- Water provided, but bring your own snacks.

Book before 30 Sept and get £2 off!

Tickets: £8 each

34 Going ▼

---

1 Read the adverts. Match the headings with the adverts.

Autumn Fair   Street Art Workshop
Relaxation Workshop

2 Read the adverts again. Match the question with the event.
Which event ...
1 offers food in the price of the ticket?
2 is only for teenagers and young adults?
3 includes a competition?
4 costs less if you buy your tickets early?
5 offers evening entertainment?
6 suggests you wear something comfortable?

3 Work in pairs. Discuss which event you would like to go to and why.

4 🔊 **1.8** Listen to the dialogue between Ben and Amy. Answer the questions.
1 Which event do they want to go to?
2 Why can't they go to it?
3 What's Ben going to do?

5 🔊 **1.9** Listen to the second dialogue. Complete the sentences.
1 Ben and Amy went to the workshop because ... .
2 Ben and Amy don't feel ... .
3 Ben isn't wearing ... .

6 💡 **GET CREATIVE** Work in pairs or small groups. You are reporters and went to one of the events in the adverts. Write a news report. Choose one person to read it to the class.

SPEAKING
Talking about a past event

I can ask and answer questions about past events.

1 🔊 **1.10** Listen and read. What did Caleb do at the weekend?

Olivia:	Hi, Caleb. How was your weekend?
Caleb:	It was amazing, thanks. I went to a drum workshop.
Olivia:	How did you find out about it?
Caleb:	I read about it online. I used to play the drums. I miss it, so I decided to go when I saw the advert for the workshop.
Olivia:	That's cool. What was it like?
Caleb:	It was very chilled. I kept making mistakes at first, but after a while I felt more confident.
Olivia:	Who did you go with?
Caleb:	No one. I went by myself.
Olivia:	What did you like most about it?
Caleb:	The final performance. Anyway Olivia, what about your weekend?

2 🔊 **1.11** Listen and repeat the **Useful language**.

Useful language

Asking
How was your weekend / holiday?
How did you find out / hear about it?
What was it like?
Who did you go with?
What did you like most about it?

Answering
It was amazing / brilliant / tiring.
I saw an advert / a poster.
It was chilled / interesting / relaxing.
I went with my brother / by myself.
The final performance / entertainment / music.

3 🔊 **1.12** Copy and complete the dialogue with words from the **Useful language** box. Listen and check.

Amy:	Hi, Nathan. ¹... Friday night?
Nathan:	It was fantastic. I saw the band competition in the park.
Amy:	Who ²... with?
Nathan:	I went with my older brother. He's really into music.
Amy:	³... hear about it?
Nathan:	I ⁴... a poster at school. I used to be in a band, so a local competition was interesting.
Amy:	Of course. And ⁵... the bands like?
Nathan:	Some were brilliant. One band was disappointing because the singer forgot his words.
Amy:	What ⁶... about it?
Nathan:	The food! The burgers were amazing!

4 Work in pairs. Prepare a new dialogue. Follow the steps in the **Speaking plan**.

Speaking plan

Prepare
› Choose one of the situations:
  • a local festival
  • a sports competition
  • a rock concert
  • a school talent show
› Make notes about the event.
› When was it? How did you hear about it? What was it like?

Speak
› Practise your dialogue.
› Use phrases from the **Useful language** box.
› Act your dialogue without notes.
› Swap roles and choose a new event.

Reflect
› Did you use adjectives to describe the experience?
› How can you improve next time?

👁 Now play *Keep moving!*

⏩ **FAST FINISHER**
You went to a festival and met an old friend. Write three sentences about it.

LS Language summary: Unit 1 **SB** p. 127

REAL CULTURE!

A museum with a difference

I can evaluate sources of information.

a Frank's BIG IDEA

♦ Nineteenth century
During the nineteenth century, there were many farms and coal mines in the north-east of England.

♦ 1950s
Frank Atkinson was the director of a traditional museum in the north-east of England, but he realized that traditional ways of life were disappearing, so he decided to create a new open-air museum. He wanted to show the lives of ordinary farmers and coal miners and their families, so he started to collect old objects. To do this, he asked local people for any objects, small or large. These included everyday objects and even old homes, buildings and a steam train!

♦ 1970s
Over the next few years, Frank moved miners' homes, a station, shops and a school, to a place called Beamish. He finally opened 'Beamish, the Living Museum of the North of England', in 1971.

♦ Now
Today, over 700,000 people a year visit Beamish open-air museum. To make Frank's idea come alive, there are actors in costumes in many of the buildings, so visitors can ask them questions about life in the 1820s, the 1900s and the 1940s. It's a great way to find out about daily lives in the past.

b Rate your visit

 ★★★★★

It was a fantastic experience! The Agriculture Festival was a memorable event. We saw lots of farm animals and everybody had a great time, including grandparents and small children.

 ★★★★☆

We liked the mining ponies most! We also enjoyed seeing the miners' houses and the old school. The only disappointing thing was the long queue for the fish and chips.

 ★★★☆☆

An exciting museum with lots to explore. The 1900s town was my favourite part. Unfortunately, we arrived at 2.45 p.m., so we only had two hours there. We took some great photos, but we didn't have time to see everything.

c Profile   Messages   Board

Local residents remember ...

I used to keep a diary when I was working in the mine. People think mines are cold, but it's very hot ... about 38°C! **Harold**

When I was young, my great grandad told amazing stories about ponies that used to work in the mine when he was a miner. In 1913, about 70,000 ponies worked in UK mines to help bring the coal out. **Flora**

My grandfather used to work on the trams as a ticket collector. He loved his job and he made a scrapbook with some old tickets in it. I still have that scrapbook! **James**

1 Look at the pictures of museums. Which two show ...
- a traditional museum?
- an open-air museum?

2 Work in pairs and talk about the differences between these two types of museums.

3 🔊 1.13 Read and listen to the sources of information on an open-air museum (a–c). Match each source to a description.

people's memories   facts   online reviews

4 Which source of information, a, b or c, mentions these things?
1 People you can ask questions about the museum.
2 A personal experience of a very difficult job.
3 The way local people helped to start the museum.
4 Feeling disappointed about waiting.
5 How people travelled in the nineteenth century.
6 A large family group having fun.
7 Not having enough time to do something.

5 Read the sources of information again and answer the questions.
1 Where did people work in north-east England in the nineteenth century?
2 Why did Frank Atkinson decide to open a museum?
3 What did Frank move to Beamish to create his museum?
4 Why are there actors in costumes in Beamish?
5 What jobs do people remember their family members doing?
6 What time does the museum close?

6 Work in groups. Which source do you think is most useful for people who want to learn about Beamish before they visit? Order them 1–3 and explain your reasons.

7 **Word Power** Some verbs and nouns often go together, for example, *tell stories*. In the sources, find verbs which go with these nouns.

... a diary   ... objects   ... some photos
... a scrapbook   ... time

8 🔍 **FIND OUT** Beamish shows what life was like in the 1900s. What was life like in your town in the 1900s? What jobs did people do and what were the local industries?

9 🌐 **COMPARE CULTURES** An English-speaking friend wants to visit a museum in your country. In groups, choose a museum. Explain what kind of things your friend can see or do there.

👁 Now watch the culture video.

» **FAST FINISHER**
Think of an old object to donate to a museum. Describe it. Who did it belong to? How old is it? What is it like?

A special memory

WRITING A story

I can write about a special event in the past.

1 Read Luna's story. What did she learn to do?

AN UNFORGETTABLE DAY

When I was fourteen, I had a brilliant birthday.

On the day, I woke up at 6 a.m. because I was excited to see my present. However, my parents were still sleeping. While I was waiting for them, I went into the living room. There was just a card on the table, so I felt a bit disappointed. Just then, Mum and Dad came into the room. After that, I opened the card. Inside was a voucher for unicycle lessons at a circus school. I was really surprised!

Later on, I went for my first unicycle lesson. I didn't feel confident at first, so I fell off a lot. After a while, my knees hurt, but every time I fell off I got back on. At the beginning, the teacher held my arm while I cycled. Eventually, I cycled on my own. It was an unforgettable day because it was great fun and I learned to do something new!

2 Answer the questions about Luna's story.
1. What was the memorable event?
2. What did Luna see on the table?
3. How did Luna feel when she opened her present?
4. Why did Luna's knees hurt?
5. Why was it an unforgettable day?

3 Look at the **Useful language**. How do you say these expressions in your language?

Useful language
Time phrases

On the day, I was … | At the beginning, …
Just then, … | Later on, …
After that, … | Eventually, …
After a while, …

4 Read the **Look!** box. Find examples of each connector in the story. Which ones have a comma (,) before them?

Look! Connectors
Connecting similar ideas: *and*
Connecting different ideas: *However, but*
Giving reasons: *so, because*

5 Complete the sentences with the correct connector.
1. I wanted to watch TV, … my dad was watching football.
2. My favourite team was playing, … I decided to watch the match.
3. The score was 1–1 at half time. …, we won 2–1.
4. Dad made me a cake … it was my birthday.
5. We all enjoyed the match … we ordered pizzas to celebrate our win after it finished.

6 Read the advert for a competition and make notes for each question.

BARTON SCHOOL WRITING COMPETITION

We want to hear all about an unforgettable day or special memory.

Was it a special event?
How old were you?
What happened?
What adjectives best describe it?

Upload your story here. You can share your photos, too. There are two cinema tickets for the best story!

7 Write a story about an unforgettable day or a favourite memory. Follow the steps in the **Writing plan**.

Writing plan

Prepare
> Write notes about your special day. Use the questions in the advert.

Write
> Organize your ideas into two or three paragraphs.
> Use the expressions from the **Useful language** box.

Reflect
> Check your grammar: past simple and past continuous with *when* and *while*.
> Check your use of connectors and time phrases.
> Check your spelling.

W Writing summary: WB p. 84   **E** Exams: Unit 1 SB p. 118   **LS** Language summary: Unit 1 SB p. 127

Time to go! 2

Vocabulary: Verbs for travel and holidays; Nouns for travel
Grammar: Present perfect with *ever/never*; Present perfect with *just, already, yet*
Speaking: Asking for help and information
Writing: An email

VOCABULARY Verbs for travel and holidays

I can use verbs for travel and holidays.

1 🔊 **2.1** Read the web page and comments. Choose the correct verbs to complete the sentences. Listen and check.

About | **Blog** | Destinations | Popular | Reviews | 👤 Log in SEARCH 🔍

Holiday habits

In the UK, 55% of people take a holiday in their own country. 'Staycations' and short breaks are more popular than ever.

Do you hate getting ready to go away? Long, annoying queues at the airport? You aren't the only one. Many families don't want to ¹ **go abroad** / **set off**. Instead, they ² **relax** / **plan** a holiday at home.

And why not? It's a great chance to ³ **explore** / **return** your own town or local area. You can ⁴ **book** / **pack** a small day bag and you don't have to worry whether the train or plane ⁵ **departs** / **stays** on time. You can have fun all day and ⁶ **arrive** / **relax** with friends in the evening.

What sort of holidays do you enjoy?

Comments

I love to ⁷ **stay** / **go abroad** at my gran's in the country. The only problem is there's no Wi-Fi. CJ

Sometimes family trips are hard work! I'd like to go to a festival with my friends. You have to be quick to ⁸ **book** / **depart** tickets for the popular ones. Harry

I like weekends away, but my dad always wants to ⁹ **unpack** / **set off** early. Sometimes we get up at 5 a.m. 😒 I need my sleep! Suzanna

My uncle's house is great because he's got his own pool. The problem is, it's about 200 kilometres away, so we're often tired when we ¹⁰ **arrive** / **explore**. Charlie

Short breaks are a good idea, but the first thing I do when we ¹¹ **return** / **plan** is see my friends. I never ¹² **pack** / **unpack** my bags the same day! Annie

Share | Like | Comment

2 Complete the questions with verbs from Exercise 1. Ask and answer in pairs.

When you go away, do you …
plan a music playlist for the journey?
1 … too many clothes?
2 … at least one new place?
3 … tickets for a local event?
4 … in the same place for a few days?
5 … with interesting souvenirs?

3 Copy the list and write verbs from Exercise 1 next to the nouns. Which verbs and nouns are the same?

arrive ▶ arrival
1 … ▶ booking
2 … ▶ departure
3 … ▶ exploration
4 … ▶ packing
5 … ▶ plan
6 … ▶ stay
7 … ▶ relaxation

4 🔍 **FIND OUT** The Transoceánica is the world's longest bus route. Which two cities does it connect? How long is the journey in hours? How long is the route in kilometres?

 Now watch the vlog.

» FAST FINISHER
Write about what you like and dislike about travel.

I love travelling by train because I can go to sleep!

LS Language summary: Unit 2 SB p. 128

Picture perfect

READING

I can find specific detail in a blog post.

◀ Blog

>>>> This week's blog post is from BiancaB in London.

Vacation? ▶ 'Fake-ation'!

My brother, Enzo

Friday evening

Have you ever visited family in another country?
I've never been abroad, but I'd love to visit my cousins. My aunt and uncle live in Barbados and my older brother, Enzo, is getting ready for a big adventure there. Enzo's never flown before. He's packed his bags and posted a photo of them online. His friends have sent goodbye messages, too.

Saturday afternoon

So, the flight departed on time and now it's arrived in Barbados, but Enzo is still in the UK. He didn't book a ticket and he hasn't gone to the Caribbean. Why not?

Well, Enzo is a student at art college and he's planned a fake holiday as a design project. In real life, our whole family is staying with my grandparents in Wales this week, but his friends don't know that ... shh!

Enzo's been in Grandad's study all afternoon. He's using a photo-editing app to put himself in photos of places in Barbados. He wants to create a new photo every day and post it online, but he's never tried to make edited photos look real before and it isn't easy!

Sunday

Today, my brother showed me an article about Zilla van den Born, a design student from the Netherlands. Zilla created a fake trip to Thailand. She posted updates while she 'was travelling in Asia'. In fact, she didn't leave home, but friends believed she was abroad. Zilla showed that a picture-perfect reality is often an illusion, especially on social media. Don't believe everything you see and read!

Tuesday evening

Have you ever felt bad about your online posts? Enzo's made some fantastic fake photos, but his friends have guessed that they aren't real, so he's told them the truth. Some people were unhappy, but most of them understood the reason for his 'fake-ation'.

A rainforest experience

New friends

1 Look at the blog post. What's unusual about the pictures of Enzo?

2 🔊 **2.2** Read and listen to the blog post and check your answer. Were you right?

3 Read the blog post again. Answer the questions.
1 Who is getting ready for a big adventure?
2 What are Bianca and her family doing this week?
3 Why is Enzo using a photo-editing app?
4 Where did Enzo get the idea for his project?
5 What did Zilla create?
6 In your opinion, how did Enzo's friends guess his photos were fake?

4 **Word Power** Find all the place names in the blog post. Make a list of more place names in English.

FUN FACT

Is this an early example of photo editing? Look carefully at the bodies. They are the same!

1850s John Calhoun

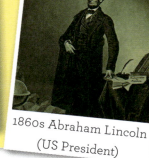
1860s Abraham Lincoln (US President)

GRAMMAR Present perfect with ever/never, been/gone

I can use the present perfect with *ever/never* and *been/gone*.

👁 Now watch the grammar animation.

Look! **Present perfect: been/gone**
The verb *go* has two past participles, *been* and *gone*.
She's **been** to Rio. (she went to a place and returned)
She's **gone** to Rio. (she went to a place and is there now)

1 Copy and complete the grammar box with the past participle of the verbs *fly*, *feel* and *visit*.

Questions
Have you/we/they ever [1]... bad about your online posts?
Has he/she/it ever [2]... family in another country?

Statements
I/You/We/They have never [3]... before.
He/She/It has never **done** that before.

Rules
1 We use *ever* in questions with the present perfect to ask if something has happened at some time in the past.
2 We use *never* in affirmative statements to mean at no time in the past.

2 A reporter has written questions for Lena, a wildlife photographer. Copy and complete the questions with the correct form of each verb. Add answers.

Have you ever ...	Lena
... (explore) the Brazilian rainforest?	✓
Have you ever explored the Brazilian rainforest? Yes, I have.	
1 ... (take) photos of a jaguar?	✗
2 ... (sleep) in a tent in the rainforest?	✓
3 ... (see) a howler monkey?	✗
4 ... (post) your photos online?	✓
5 ... (use) a photo-editing app?	✗

3 Complete the notes from Lena's interview using her answers from Exercise 2.

4 Complete the sentences with *been* or *gone*.
1 Have you ever ... to the USA?
2 My sister is very tired this evening. She's ... on a school trip to a museum today.
3 I've never ... to that restaurant. Is it good?
4 I don't know where they've ... . Why don't you call them?
5 Have you ever ... to the new cinema in town?
6 Ali isn't at football practice tonight. He's ... to a birthday party.

5 In your notebooks, write questions with *Have you ever ...?* Ask and answer the questions in pairs.

explore / a rainforest? see / a wild animal?
eat / Italian ice cream? be / on a school trip?
buy / souvenir? take / a funny selfie?

Have you ever explored a rainforest?

Yes, I have.

No, I've never explored a rainforest.

Lena **has explored** the Brazilian rainforest many times, but she [1] ... never ... photos of a jaguar. She [2] ... in a tent in the rainforest. She [3] ... never ... a howler monkey, but she's heard one. They're very loud! Lena [4] ... her photos online on her blog, but she [5] ... never ... a photo-editing app.

6 🎯 **COMPARE CULTURES**
For visitors to the UK, the Tower of London is a popular location for photographs. What locations in your country do visitors like to photograph?

» FAST FINISHER
Write sentences for a fake travel blog. Use *I've been* / *I haven't been* to talk about different places.

Has the train left?

VOCABULARY and LISTENING Nouns for travel

I can identify key information in short dialogues and announcements.

1 Look at the picture. Can you see any unusual objects?

2 🔊 2.3 Match the words with the letters. Listen and check.

> announcement   arrivals board   departures board
> information desk   ~~lost property office~~   queue
> seat   taxi rank   the Underground
> ticket machine   trolley   wheelie bag

3 Complete the tips with words from Exercise 2.

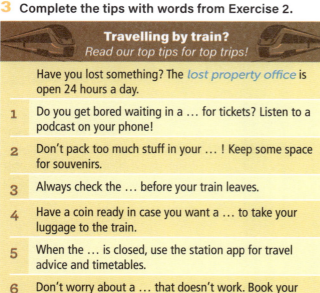

Have you lost something? The *lost property office* is open 24 hours a day.

1 Do you get bored waiting in a … for tickets? Listen to a podcast on your phone!
2 Don't pack too much stuff in your … ! Keep some space for souvenirs.
3 Always check the … before your train leaves.
4 Have a coin ready in case you want a … to take your luggage to the train.
5 When the … is closed, use the station app for travel advice and timetables.
6 Don't worry about a … that doesn't work. Book your tickets online.

4 🔊 2.4 Listen to the dialogues and announcements. Answer the questions.
1 What does Felix need?
   a A wheelie bag.
   b A trolley.
   c Some money for snacks.
2 Ellie has left her phone at the
   a information desk.
   b lost property office.
   c ticket machine.
3 Why is Alice very hungry?
   a She forgot to bring something to eat.
   b She only had fruit for breakfast.
   c She didn't have time to make lunch.
4 The problem with the Cardiff train is that
   a it has no food or drink.
   b the departure time has changed.
   c there are no seats.
5 The man
   a has bought the wrong ticket from the ticket machine.
   b has taken the wrong train.
   c has taken somebody's seat.

LS Language summary: Unit 2 SB p. 128

GRAMMAR Present perfect with *just, already, yet*

 I can use the present perfect with *just*, *already* and *yet*.

👁 Now watch the grammar animation.

1 Read the grammar box. Complete the rules with *just*, *already* and *yet*.

Affirmative	Negative
I've **just** bought this ticket.	I haven't found my phone **yet**.
He's **already** found a trolley.	The train hasn't left **yet**.
They've **just** announced our train.	

Questions	Short answers
Have you eaten **yet**?	Yes, I have. / No, I haven't.
Have they announced our train **yet**?	Yes, they have. / No, they haven't.

Rules

We use ¹… in affirmative sentences for things that have happened sooner than we expected or before a particular time.

We use ²… in negative sentences and questions to talk about things that we expect to happen.

We use ³… for actions that happened a very short time ago.

2 Complete the sentences with *just*, *already* or *yet*.

Have you called a taxi *yet*? It's time to leave.
1 We can't pack another bag. We've … packed six!
2 This shop has great souvenirs. I've … found this hat!
3 There's Dad. He's … come out of the ticket office.
4 They haven't announced our flight … .
5 Has Mia finished her project …?

3 Complete the sentences with the correct form of the verb.

Ana and Si *have just arrived* (just/arrive) at school.
1 … (Mum/book/yet) the train tickets …?
2 … (we/not see/yet) the Eiffel Tower … .
3 Mr York … (already/plan) the next school trip.
4 Jake … (just/leave) to go to the airport.
5 Alice … (not set off/yet).

4 PRONUNCIATION *have/has*: strong and weak forms

🔊 **2.5** Listen and repeat.

strong forms	weak forms
have /hæv/	have /həv/
has /hæz/	has /həz/

5 🔊 **2.6** Listen. When do we use strong forms and weak forms? Listen again and repeat.

6 In your notebook, write questions and short answers. In pairs, take it in turns to ask and answer.

you / unpack / your bag / yet? ✓
Have you unpacked your bag yet? Yes, I have.
1 you / use / the Underground / yet? ✗
2 you / see / my holiday photos / yet? ✗
3 you / finish / your project / yet? ✓
4 you and your friends / try / that new café / yet? ✓
5 your parents / return from their trip / yet? ✗

7 🔊 **2.7** Complete the travel blog with the correct form of the words in the box. Listen and check.

already/do   explore/yet   ~~already/have~~
just/organize   just/arrive   not meet/yet
not unpack/yet

Travels with Jacob

Hi, and welcome to my travel blog. For me, the best bit of any holiday is being with friends or meeting new people. As you know, I *'ve already had* some cool adventures. This week, I'm at an activity camp with some good friends. We ¹… after a ten-hour coach journey. I didn't sleep much, so I'm really tired. I ²…, but I think I've forgotten my swimming things – typical!

The camp is in the mountains and our teacher ³… a mountain bike ride for tomorrow. I can't wait! There's another group of students our age, but the two groups ⁴…! I'm glad we've got a week here to get to know each other.

What about you? ⁵… somewhere new … this summer? Or are you having fun at home? Tell me what you ⁶… with your friends or what you plan to do!

» **FAST FINISHER**

Write three sentences about your day. Use *already*, *just* and *yet*.

Can you help us?

READING and LISTENING

I can use a map to get information.

1 Look at the map. What kind of things can you do in Brighton?

2 Find the places in **bold** on the map. Match the questions with the answers.

1. What can you do on Brighton **Pier**?
2. Can we book tickets here for the **i360**?
3. What are **The Lanes**?
4. What's the **Royal Pavilion** like?

a They're small streets with interesting old buildings.
b It used to be a palace. It's a short walk from the pier.
c Yes, of course. The views from the top of the tower are amazing.
d There are fairground rides and cafés. It's a fantastic place for a walk.

3 ◆ 2.8 Listen to the dialogues. Check your answers to Exercise 2.

4 ◆ 2.9 Complete the phrases from the dialogues. Listen and check.

  A: *Which way* is it to the pier?
  B: It's on the seafront. It isn't *far*.
1 A: Can you help us? ... a map of Brighton, please.
  B: Of course. Here you are.
2 A: What ... to do there?
  B: You can enjoy the shops or just explore the area.
3 A: Can you ... on the map, please?
  B: Of course. It's just there.

Brighton Pier

SPEAKING Asking for help and information

I can ask for help and information about a place.

1 🔊 **2.10 Listen and read. What are they looking for?**

Lara:	It's five o'clock. Time to catch the bus.
Milo:	But you've both already got your souvenirs and I haven't bought one yet. Wait two minutes, OK?
Yana:	OK, but hurry. Which way is the bus stop? Let's ask someone.
Lara:	Excuse me. Can you help us? We're looking for the bus stop in Churchill Square. Do you know where it is?
Man:	Sure. It's just down that street.
Yana:	How far is it? Can you show me on this map, please?
Man:	Of course. Here. It isn't far. It's five minutes on foot.
Yana:	Thank you. Hey, Milo! Have you bought anything yet?
Milo:	Yes. Look! I've just bought a great souvenir. A seagull!
Lara:	It's cute, but now we'd better run!

2 🔊 **2.11 Listen and repeat the Useful language.**

Useful language

Asking for help
Excuse me, which way is … ?
Can you help us?
We're looking for …
Do you know where … is?
How far is …?
Can you show me on this map?

Giving information
It's just down … street.
It isn't far.
It's … minutes on foot.
It's that way.
It's a long way.

3 🔊 **2.12 Put the dialogue in order from 1–5. Listen and check.**

a   Thank you very much.
b   I'm looking for the bus stop for the number 5 bus.
c   Excuse me. Can you help me?
d   Well, it isn't far. It's that way, in front of the cinema. It's ten minutes on foot.
e   Yes, of course. What's the problem?

4 Work in pairs. Prepare a new dialogue. Follow the steps in the **Speaking plan**.

Speaking plan

Prepare
› You are outside your school. Some tourists ask for information about one of these places:
  • a place to buy food or drinks
  • a bus stop or train station
  • a place to stay
› Choose one of the places.
› Make notes for your dialogue. Use phrases from the **Useful language** box.

Speak
› Practise your dialogue.
› Act out your dialogue without notes.
› Swap roles and choose a new place.

Reflect
› Did you ask politely using *Excuse me* and saying *Thank you*?
› How can you improve next time?

Now play *Keep moving!*

⏩ **FAST FINISHER**
How many words can you make from the letters in *Brighton Pier*?
gone, …

LS Language summary: Unit 2 SB p. 128

REAL CULTURE!

Something to take home

I can understand an article about souvenirs.

Souvenirs
(and why they matter)

Have family members ever given you a souvenir from their holiday? Maybe you found something unusual on a trip? In most holiday resorts, there are lots of souvenir shops selling everything from cheap key rings, fridge magnets and pencil cases, to more expensive jewellery and handmade chocolates.

The first souvenirs

Collecting souvenirs isn't new. In 1786, Thomas Jefferson, the third president of the USA, visited William Shakespeare's birthplace in Stratford-upon-Avon, England. Historians say that Jefferson saw an old, wooden chair where the writer used to sit. He and other tourists on the tour cut off a piece of wood and took it home!

Why we like souvenirs

So, why do people like souvenirs? Most of us take hundreds of photos when we're away, so why do we need a silly hat or a model of Buckingham Palace? A souvenir is often a very personal choice. It reminds us of our travels. It can also be a talking point. When friends ask about it, we can't wait to describe where we bought it, who we were with and what we were doing. We enjoy remembering and talking about our holiday. Sometimes the story behind the souvenir is better than the souvenir itself.

Culture and history

Souvenirs can also tell us a lot about culture and history. We've searched around the world for some great souvenirs. How about an inukshuk from Canada? These stones were like a GPS system for the people of the Arctic region. They've become a symbol of hope and friendship around the world. Fabric from India represents the colours and costumes of the country. A baseball cap is useful against the hot sun. It's also a reminder of America's national sport.

However, sometimes the best souvenirs don't have to cost a lot. They can be old bus tickets, menus from your favourite restaurant (ask first!) or some leftover currency. What's your favourite souvenir?

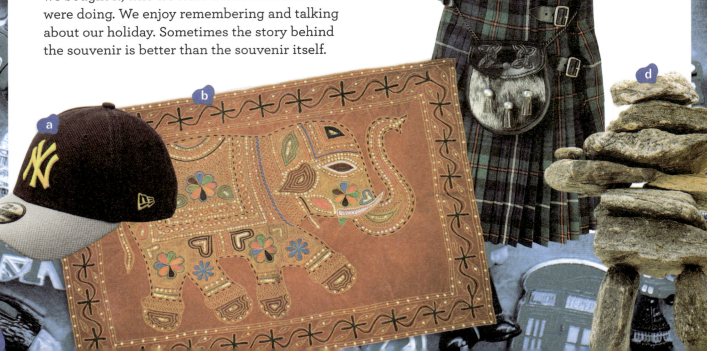

2

1. In pairs, look at the pictures of souvenirs from around the world. Which ones do you like most and why?

2. Read the text and look at pictures a–d. Which three souvenir ideas are in the text?

3. 🔊 2.13 Read and listen. Answer the questions.
   1. What sort of souvenirs do you find in holiday resorts?
   2. How did Thomas Jefferson get his souvenir?
   3. Why do people like souvenirs?
   4. What does an inukshuk represent?
   5. Why is a baseball cap a useful souvenir?

4. Look at the pictures of other souvenirs from around the world. Match the pictures with the country they come from.

   Russia   Japan   Australia   Peru

5. 🔊 2.14 Listen to the people describing their favourite souvenirs. Which souvenirs from Exercise 4 do the people mention?

6. 🔊 2.14 Listen again and answer the questions.
   1. Who gave Mike his souvenir?
   2. What do you do with a boomerang?
   3. What was Sally's perfect souvenir?
   4. Where did she lose it?
   5. Which colour is Claudia's maneki-neko?
   6. What does it mean?

7. 💭 **THINK CRITICALLY** Do you think Thomas Jefferson was right or wrong to take the wood?

   I think he was wrong because he didn't pay for it.

   I think it was OK because …

8. **Word Power** Find examples of compound nouns in the text. They can have one or two words.
   holiday resort, …

9. Complete the sentences with compound nouns from the text.
   1. I'm walking home because I've lost my … .
   2. My favourite … is Cancún in Mexico. The beaches are amazing.
   3. We went to Alcalá de Henares, the … of Cervantes.
   4. Can I borrow a pen, please? I've left my … at home.

10. **GET CREATIVE** In groups, choose a country. Research a souvenir from that country. Follow steps 1–5.
    1. Decide what the souvenir is and where it is from.
    2. Say what it shows about the country.
    3. Discuss who might buy it.
    4. Explain why you chose the souvenir.
    5. Present your findings to the class.

FUN FACT Are you looking for an unusual souvenir? How about a tin of fresh air from New York? Yes, you guessed it: this joke souvenir is really an empty tin … and it comes from Czechia!

👁 Now watch the culture video.

⏩ **FAST FINISHER**
Write a list of ideas for souvenirs from your town. Think of things people can eat, wear or take to school.

Holiday news

WRITING An email

I can write an email with my holiday news.

1 Look at the holiday activities in the images. What do you enjoy doing most/least? Why?

2 Read the email and answer the questions.
 1 What activities has Emma already done?
 2 What have Emma and her cousins planned?

Hi Noah,

Thanks for your message. I've just seen your photos. It looks as though you're having fun. Have you swum in the lake yet?

I'm having such a great time at my cousins' house. We arrived a week ago by train. It was a long journey and I didn't have a seat for the first hour. It was so annoying! I'm sharing a room with my cousins. I haven't slept much because we play computer games until late and talk a lot. I've already met a lot of their friends and we've explored the area on bikes. We've just organized a camping trip for the weekend. The only problem is the weather. It's really hot! I haven't brought many summer clothes.

Apart from that, we've been to the beach. I found a brilliant souvenir shop. They sell such cool fridge magnets and I've bought one for you.

I can't believe the holiday is going so quickly! Hope to see you soon.

Love,
Emma xx

3 Read the email again. Copy and complete the mind map.

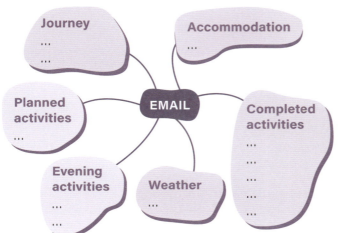

4 Look at the **Useful language** box. How do you say these expressions in your language? Which expressions does Emma use?

> **Useful language**
> **Responding to news and asking about news**
> It was great to hear from you.
> Thanks for your message/news.
> Have you ... yet?
>
> **Giving your news**   **Finishing the email**
> I'm having such a great time.   That's all for now.
> I've just arrived in ...   Hope to see you soon.
> Apart from that, ...

5 Read the **Look!** box. Find an example of each word in the email.

> **Look!** really, so, such
>
> We use **really** or **so** with an adjective or adverb:
> It's **really** cold.
> These two weeks are going **so** fast!
> We usually use **such** (a/an) with a noun phrase (an adjective and a noun together):
> I'm having **such a** great time.
> They sell **such** cool T-shirts.

6 Copy and complete the sentences with really/so or such.
 The train arrived really/so late.
 1 The technology museum was ... interesting.
 2 I've just had ... a good holiday.
 3 I was ... tired after my long journey.
 4 It was ... an uncomfortable seat!
 5 That was ... a good trip.

7 Write an email to your friend. Write about what you have done so far on your holiday and what souvenirs you have bought. Follow the steps in the **Writing plan**.

> **Writing plan**
>
> **Prepare**
> › Write notes about your holiday. Use Exercise 3 to help you.
>
> **Write**
> › Ask your friend about his/her holiday.
> › Give news about your holiday. Use your notes to help you.
> › Use the expressions from the **Useful language** box.
> › Think about how to end the email.
>
> **Reflect**
> › Check your grammar: present perfect and just/already/yet.
> › Check your use of really, so and such.

Eat up!

Vocabulary: Food and drink adjectives; Cooking
Grammar: Present perfect, How long ...?, for and since; Past simple
Speaking: Expressing preferences
Writing: A description

VOCABULARY   Food and drink adjectives

I can describe the taste and texture of food and drink.

1. Work in pairs. Look at the pictures. When do people eat snacks like these?

2. 🔊 3.1 Read and listen to the article. Then match the pictures with four of the snack descriptions.

SNACK ATTACK!

School's just finished and you want a snack – something small to keep you going until dinner. We asked you to share your favourite snacks.

 I always have natural yoghurt. I love **creamy** Greek yoghurt with fruit in it. Some people think it is **sour**, but I think it's delicious. **Milla**, *Finland*

 Definitely curry fish balls with chilli sauce. It's quite **spicy** and a little **salty**, too. Sometimes I just have some **crispy** prawn crackers. **Chan**, *Hong Kong*

 I try to wait for dinner, but when I'm really hungry I have some **crunchy raw** carrots with hummus. **Jess**, *UK*

 I like a **savoury** snack. I love **fresh** bread with avocado and salt and pepper on it, but not so it's too **salty**. It's simple, but so good. **Vicente**, *Chile*

 My favourite snack is a watermelon ice lolly. It's **sweet** and healthy. It's **frozen** fruit on a stick and it tastes great on a hot day. **Akinari**, *Japan*

3. 🔊 3.2 Read and listen to the adjectives. How do you say them in your language?

| creamy | crispy | crunchy | fresh | frozen |
| raw | salty | savoury | sour | spicy | sweet |

Look! *savoury* and *salty*

Savoury food is not sweet. It has salt or spice in it.
Salty means that salt is the main flavour.

4. Complete the sentences with the correct adjective from Exercise 3.

   I was thirsty after eating the *salty* soup.
   1. They buy ... fruit and vegetables at the market.
   2. This soup is really ... . I think it has some milk in it.
   3. After a .... curry, I ate yoghurt to cool my mouth!
   4. We keep some ... desserts in the freezer.
   5. I prefer ... snacks to sweets and biscuits.

5. In pairs, describe these foods with adjectives from Exercise 3.

| a green salad | an apple | chicken curry |
| chicken soup | chocolate | sorbet |

6. Discuss the questions with your partner.
   1. What is your favourite after-school snack? Why?
   2. Do you prefer sweet or savoury snacks? Why?

7. **COMPARE CULTURES** In groups, write a list of snacks that are popular in your country. How would you describe the snacks to an English-speaking friend?

 Now watch the vlog.

≫ FAST FINISHER

Beginning with **C**rea**m Y**oghu**r T**omatoe**S** ..., use the last letter to start a new food word and make a word snake. Use adjectives and nouns. How many words can you make?

LS Language summary: Unit 3 **SB** p. 129

Silent snacks

READING **I can** use pictures to predict what a text is about.

1 **Look at the pictures and the title of the article. Discuss the questions.**
   1 Why does the girl have her hands over her ears?
   2 What is the connection between the two pictures?

2 🔊 3.3 **Listen to six sounds. What food or drink do you think you hear?**

3 🔊 3.4 **Read and listen to the text. Which food from Exercise 2 does the text mention?**

SHHH, IT'S TIME FOR SOME QUIET FOOD!

You're enjoying a film at the cinema. Then someone nearby starts eating crisps. You hear the noise of the bag, then *crunch, crunch*. You start to feel annoyed, and after a few minutes you can't follow the film. Does this sound familiar? You're not alone. Claire has known this feeling since she was little.

How long have you felt like this?
I've had this problem for ten years. It's called misophonia. People with this condition are sensitive to noise. My dad's got it, too. He explained to me that some people feel angry when they hear people eat certain foods. For me, it's the noise of people eating crispy foods, but for others it's the sound of someone eating a juicy orange or sweets. The packaging is part of the problem – crisp packets are especially annoying!

Why is the cinema so difficult for you?
I think there are two reasons. People eat lots of noisy snacks in the cinema such as crisps, nuts and popcorn. It's also difficult to get away from the noise unless you leave the cinema. I love the smell of popcorn, but I hate the sound of it!

Has this stopped you going to the cinema?
Yes. I haven't been to a cinema since the summer.

So, what's the answer?
Well, some food companies are trying to help. One company has stopped using plastic and has developed fabric bags. It has also invented some new snacks, like chocolate balls that you can eat quietly. The chocolate looks good and it tastes great. And best of all, these snacks are quiet!

4 **Read the article again. Answer the questions.**
   1 When did Claire's problem begin?
   2 What's the name of Claire's problem?
   3 Why did Claire's dad recognize her feelings?
   4 What foods can cause problems for other people?
   5 Which sounds make Claire angry at a cinema?
   6 When did Claire last go to the cinema?
   7 How has one company changed its packaging?
   8 What new snack has been developed?

5 **Word Power** The verbs *look*, *feel* and *smell* are verbs of the senses. Find two more in the article and complete the sentences.

   Those biscuits *look* really good with all that decoration.
   1 Mmm, something ... good. What is it? Are you baking a chocolate cake?
   2 My hands ... cold. Where are my gloves?
   3 Do you think this soup ... too salty?
   4 Listen to Eva sing. She ... amazing.
   5 My new shirt ... very soft on my skin.

6 💭 **THINK CRITICALLY** Work in groups. Discuss the statement 'People shouldn't eat or drink in the cinema'. Do you agree? Why/Why not?

GRAMMAR Present perfect with *How long ...?*, *for* and *since*

I can use the present perfect with *How long ...?*, *for* and *since*.

◉ Now watch the grammar animation.

1 Copy the grammar box and complete the examples with a phrase from the box.

| for ten years | have you felt |
| since she was little | since the summer |

How long ...?, *for* and *since*

How long ¹... like this?
I **'ve had** the problem ²... .
I **haven't been** to the cinema ³... .
She **'s known** this feeling ⁴... .

Rules

We use *How long ...?* + present perfect to ask questions about the duration of a situation.

We use *for* with a period of time, e.g. *for ten years*.

We use *since* with a fixed time in the past, e.g. *since the summer*.

We can use *since* + past simple with the present perfect to describe when a situation started.

2 Complete the sentences with *for* or *since*.
1. Nathan has written a food blog ... he left college.
2. The café has served hot food ... last year.
3. I haven't eaten any sweet snacks ... two weeks.
4. My brother has baked great cakes ... he was ten.
5. I've lived in Salamanca ... I was six.
6. I've wanted to try Japanese food ... a long time.

3 Complete the sentences with the present perfect form of the verbs in brackets and *How long ...?*, *for* or *since*.

Jacob **has eaten** (eat) a lot of cake *since* he arrived.

1. We ... (know) the waiter ... a long time.
2. You ... (not drink) any water ... a few hours.
3. '... you ... (live) in this town?' 'I've lived here ... seven years.'
4. I ... (feel) sick ... I ate all that pizza.
5. '... your sister ... (be) at university?' 'She ... there ... two years.'
6. My sister ... (work) as a chef ... 2017.

4 🔍 **FIND OUT** Astronauts have to eat special food in space. What do they eat for bread?

5 Complete the food facts with the present perfect form of the verb in brackets and *for* or *since*.

The aeroplane maker Boeing *has used* (use) bags of potatoes on seats to test Wi-Fi signals on planes ¹... 2012. Potatoes and humans affect Wi-Fi signals in similar ways, so people don't have to sit on a plane for hours while they test the signals.

How long ²... (you / have) that jar of honey in your kitchen cupboard? It probably ³... (not be) there ⁴... a very long time. However, archaeologists have recently discovered some ancient honey. The honey ⁵... (survive) in ceramic pots ⁶... more than 5,500 years and you can still eat it!

Researchers think people in Mexico ⁷... (use) cacao beans for food and drinks ⁸... 1900 BC. Scientists ⁹... (discover) that chocolate was a popular drink over 1,600 years ago.

6 Work in pairs. Take turns to ask and discuss the questions.
1. know your best friend
2. be a student at this school
3. live in your house
4. be at school today

How long have you known your best friend?

I've known him since I started primary school.

FUN FACT

Chefs have worn tall white hats since the sixteenth century. These hats stop hair falling into food. The height of the hat shows how much experience the chef has.

» FAST FINISHER

What food do you like/dislike? Why? How long have you liked/disliked it? Write three sentences.

LS Language summary: Unit 3 **SB** p. 129

That's unusual!

VOCABULARY and LISTENING Cooking methods and menus

I can identify specific information in an interview.

1 🔊 3.5 Match the verbs with the pictures. Listen and check.

| barbecue | bake | boil | fry | grill | microwave | roast | stir fry |

2 Read the menu. Match the pictures a–c with the food on the menu. Why are these foods unusual?

3 Read the menu again. Underline the adjective form of the verbs from Exercise 1.

4 Read the menu again. Use the correct form of the blue words to answer the questions.

What word or phrase means …
   the first part of a meal? *starter*
1 food that you eat between meals?
2 something sweet you eat after a meal?
3 a dish that wasn't bought from a shop?
4 the different things that you use to make a particular dish?
5 things that you serve with a main meal?
6 the biggest or most important part of a meal?

5 🔊 3.6 Listen to the interview about Sticky Fingers Café. How does Lily feel after cooking all day?

6 🔊 3.6 Listen again. Are the sentences true (T) or false (F)? Correct the false sentences.

   The restaurant has been open for six years.
   F – It has been open for six months.
1 The restaurant is popular with students.
2 The dishes have unusual ingredients.
3 The reporter has tried one of the hot dishes.
4 They don't serve well-known dishes.
5 Lily has made lots of cronuts today.

7 Work in pairs. Discuss the questions.
1 Which of the methods do you or your family use?
2 What food do you cook with each method?

LS Language summary: Unit 3 SB p. 129

GRAMMAR Present perfect and past simple

I can use the present perfect and the past simple.

Now watch the grammar animation.

1 Choose the correct answer to complete the rules.

Present perfect
We'**ve introduced** some new dishes.
We **haven't had** any bad reviews.

Past simple
The café **opened** six months ago.
Last night, I **didn't want** to cook.

Questions
Have you made any cronuts today?
No, I **haven't**, but I **made** 90 yesterday!

Rules
We use the present perfect to talk about recent events or past events when the time ¹ *is / is not* specified.

We use the past simple for finished actions and situations that ² *started / started and finished* at a specific time.

We often ask for information in the ³ *present perfect / past simple* and give more examples in the ⁴ *present perfect / past simple*.

2 Choose the correct answers.
1 I've made / made a cake last night.
2 Be careful! I've spilled / spilled some milk.
3 Did Ethan cook / cooked on the trip?
4 The customers were / have been happy with last night's menu.
5 Amelia has known / knew how to ride a bike since she was four.
6 Have you seen / Did you see any good films recently?
7 We've seen / saw all the Harry Potter films.

3 Complete the sentences with the present perfect or past simple form of the verbs in brackets.
  Liam *left* (leave) a few minutes ago.
1 I … (cook) dinner for us. Are you ready to eat?
2 Their restaurant … (win) a prize last month for its creative menu.
3 Gino … (not make) any meals since he finished the cookery course.
4 She doesn't want dessert yet because she … (not finish) her main course.
5 We … (order) a pizza an hour ago.
6 I … (not read) a book in English.
7 She … (arrive) this morning.

4 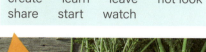 3.7 Complete the article with the present perfect or past simple form of the verbs in the box. Listen and check.

| create | learn | leave | not look |
| share | start | watch | |

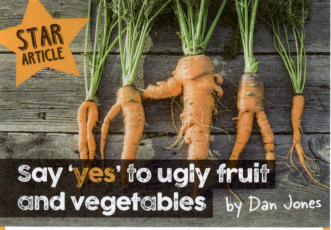

STAR ARTICLE

say 'yes' to ugly fruit and vegetables by Dan Jones

Do you eat bananas with black spots on the skin? Have you left an apple in the bowl because it ¹ … perfect? I used to be like that. Then I ² … a video at school about food waste and I ³ … that nearly 40% of the fruit and vegetables we buy end up in the bin. So last month, my brother and I ⁴ … a social media account. Over the last few weeks, we ⁵ … lots of photos of funny fruit and vegetables and the meals we made from them. More than 100 people ⁶ … us comments since we ⁷ … it, and we're getting new followers every day. We just want people to know that something that looks ugly can still taste delicious!

5 Work in pairs. Discuss the questions.
1 Have you ever bought ugly fruit or vegetables?
2 Did they taste different from perfect fruit or vegetables?

6 PRONUNCIATION /s/, /z/ and /ɪz/

3.8 Listen to how we say the endings of the following words. Copy and complete the table.

| dishes | messages | meals |
| spots | vegetables | weeks |

/s/	/z/	/ɪz/

7 3.9 Listen and check. Then add the words to the table in Exercise 6.
1 cakes   2 courses
3 customers   4 noodles
5 ingredients   6 sandwiches

» FAST FINISHER
Compare what you have eaten or drunk today with what you ate and drank at the weekend. What food did you enjoy most?

LS Language summary: Unit 3 **SB** p. 129

33

I'd prefer pizza

READING and LISTENING

I can understand information and notices about food.

a

FOOD ALLERGY WARNING

Do you have a food allergy or any special requests?

Please contact our staff so we can advise on your food choices.

b

DINING AREA FOR CUSTOMERS ONLY

Please consume only food and drink that you have bought here.

c

Natural smoothies

COFFEE SHAKE
coffee, almond milk, banana

FUNKY MONKEY
peanut butter, milk, banana, chocolate sauce

TROPICAL DREAM*
mangoes, pineapple and coconut milk

* nut-free and noticesz

d

Italian-style pasta

Gluten-free, wheat-free

Ingredients: corn and rice

Boiling time: 8–9 minutes

e

Quick Vegetarian Pizza

- Preparation time: 15 minutes
- Cooking time: 12–15 minutes

Ingredients for the base:
- 425 g flour (standard wheat flour or gluten-free)
- 1 packet yeast
- 1 teaspoon sugar
- Half teaspoon salt
- 350 ml warm water

Ingredients for the topping:
- tomatoes, cheese, olives, mushrooms

f

The Wok House

82 High Street, Kenton

Orders:
📞 020 7946 0288

Open daily 11.30 a.m. – 11.30 p.m.

Eat in / take away

Vegetarian options

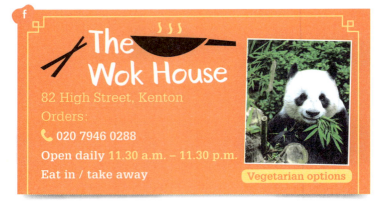

---

1 Look at the information and notices about food. Work in pairs. Discuss the questions.
  1 What is the connection between the notices and the words in the box below?

> eggs   fish   milk and cheese
> peanuts or other nuts   wheat flour

  2 Do you know anyone who has an allergy?

2 Match the text types in the box with texts a–f.

> advert   menu   notice   packaging   recipe

  a notice

3 Look at texts a–f again. Which texts tell you …
  1 the cooking method?
  2 not to eat picnics?
  3 to speak to a person who works there?
  4 the address of a restaurant?
  5 how long you need to cook something?
  6 the names of drinks?

4 🔊 3.10 Listen to three dialogues. Match them with texts a–f.

5 🔊 3.10 Listen again. What is the problem in each dialogue?

34

SPEAKING Expressing preferences

I can express my preferences.

1 Work in pairs. Look at the picture and describe what you can see. Guess what has happened.

2 🔊 3.11 Listen and read. Why can't they eat the food Silvia made?

> **Silvia:** Hi, Amy. Come in. I've made a vegetarian lasagne for you.
> **Amy:** Thank you! I haven't had lasagne for ages. What's that smell?
> **Silvia:** Oh no! I've just burned it. I'd rather eat out than eat this.
> **Amy:** Shame! I was looking forward to that.
> **Silvia:** I haven't got enough ingredients to start again. Would you rather eat out or get a takeaway?
> **Amy:** I don't mind. Actually, I'd prefer to get a takeaway.
> **Silvia:** OK then ... . Do you fancy Indian food?
> **Amy:** Well, I'd prefer pizza to be honest. Indian food is too spicy.
> **Silvia:** Have you heard of Perfect Pizza? They use really fresh ingredients. Their barbecue chicken pizza is fantastic! Or would you prefer a sweet pizza? They make a fruit pizza, too.
> **Amy:** Really? Let's order online then. But I'd rather not try sweet pizza, thanks!

3 Find phrases in the dialogue with similar meanings.

It's been a long time since I ate ... .
I haven't had (lasagne) for ages.

1 Either of the options is OK with me.
2 Would you like to have ...?
3 Do you know about ...?

4 🔊 3.12 Listen and repeat the **Useful language**.

> **Useful language**
>
> **Expressing present and future preferences**
>
> I would / I'd prefer (+ noun)
> I would / I'd prefer to (+ verb)
> I'd rather ... (+ verb + *than* ...)
> I'd rather not ... (+ verb)
> Would you rather ... (+ verb)?
> Would you prefer ... (+ noun)?
> Yes, I would. / No, I wouldn't.

5 Look at the **Useful language**. How do you say those phrases in your language?

6 🔊 3.13 Copy and complete the dialogue. Listen and check.

> **Frankie:** Do you fancy some street food?
> **Jess:** Sounds good, but I'd prefer ¹... go to Gino's Café. It's really cool.
> **Frankie:** OK, great. There are some tables inside.
> **Jess:** I ²... rather sit outside ³... go inside.
> **Frankie:** OK. The menu looks good.
> **Jess:** We could have soup. Or would you ⁴... coffee and cake?
> **Frankie:** Yes, I ⁵... . Great idea!

7 Work in pairs. Prepare a new dialogue. Follow the steps in the **Speaking plan**.

> **Speaking plan**
>
> **Prepare**
> › Decide on a situation for your dialogue.
>   • place: café, juice bar or street food stall inside or outside
>   • drink: fruit juice, coffee
>   • snack: cake, soup
> › Make notes for your dialogue.
> › Use phrases fom the **Useful language** box.
>
> **Speak**
> › Practise your dialogue.
> › Act your dialogue without notes.
> › Swap roles and change the choice of place, food and drink in your dialogue.
>
> **Reflect**
> › Did you ask about your partner's preferences and clearly express your own?
> › How can you improve next time?

 Now play *Keep moving!*

≫ FAST FINISHER

Describe two types of food that are popular in your country. Which do you prefer? Why?

LS Language summary: Unit 3 **SB** p. 129

REAL CULTURE!

International flavour

I can understand what a writer wants to say in an article.

Popular UK food:
a short guide

The history of food shows some UK favourites are not so British after all! Here some young food experts share their knowledge.

Fish and chips by Eddie Powell

1570s

Did you know there are about 10,500 fish and chip shops in the UK? Historians think that John Lees opened the first fish and chip stall in northern England in 1863. The dish quickly became a favourite with families because it was an easy meal. It was also tasty and cheap. Although it was fried food, it contained plenty of protein and vitamins.

1789

You need potatoes to make chips and they arrived in Europe in the 1570s. Where did they come from? Peru. People there started growing them thousands of years ago. What's more, the UK didn't invent chips. They came to the UK from France, where they first sold 'French fries' in 1789.

1810

Indian by Alex Smith

Chips are not the only food from abroad that has become popular with British people. Indian food, particularly curry, has been popular since the 1960s. However, not many people know that the first Indian restaurant opened in the UK before the first fish and chip shop!

1863

Saik Deen Mahomad realized that many British people would rather have spicy food than plain food, so he opened an Indian restaurant in London in 1810, which also offered home deliveries. This was a brilliant idea, and customers loved his unusual 'takeaway' service.

1908

Chinese by Leena Salomi

In 1908, *The Chinese Restaurant* opened in London. It was not the first Chinese restaurant, but it was the first one outside a Chinese neighbourhood. The most popular dish on the menu was sweet and sour pork, and this is still a best-seller today.

1958

By the 1950s, more people were trying Chinese food. When the *Lotus House* restaurant opened in London in 1958, customers used to queue in the streets. In the end, people who couldn't get a table asked for food to take away. They say this was the real beginning of 'takeaway' culture in the UK.

1960s

3

1 Look at the pie chart. Which is the most popular takeaway food in the UK? Which food is traditionally British?

2 Read the text quickly. What happened at each time on the timeline?

3 🔊 3.14 Read and listen to the text. Choose the best answer.
1 What are the experts trying to do in this text?
  a Describe some typical British restaurant meals.
  b Suggest some interesting food that visitors to the UK can try.
  c Give a short history of different UK eating habits.
2 What do we learn about chips?
  a They came to the UK from France.
  b They are thousands of years old.
  c They came from Peru.
3 Which of these facts about Indian food does the text mention?
  a Indian restaurants are older than fish and chip shops.
  b Takeaway service is traditional in India.
  c Indian food used to be popular in the 1950s.
4 Takeaway food started because people …
  a didn't enjoy sitting in restaurants.
  b wanted to eat out in the streets.
  c didn't like the restaurant queues.
5 What does the text say about Chinese restaurants?
  a The first restaurant opened in 1958.
  b They started the idea of 'takeaway' food.
  c The most popular restaurants were Chinese in the 1900s.

4 **Word Power** Work in pairs. Make a list of places where you can buy meals. Which are most popular with your class?

Indian restaurant, fish and chip shop

5 Look at the pictures. Decide which country each meal comes from and match it with a flag.

a    b

c    d

e    f

1 Kebabs    2 Tapas

3 Roast dinner    4 Bratwurst

5 Snails    6 Custard tarts

FUN FACT  Fish shops used to wrap fish and chips in newspaper because it was cheap! However, in the 1980s this changed because it was not safe to use paper covered in ink.

6 💡 **GET CREATIVE** Work in pairs or small groups. Find facts and pictures about the history of a dish in your country. Present it to the class.

👁 Now watch the culture video.

» FAST FINISHER

Some friends have invited you for a birthday meal. Would you prefer to have takeaway food or homemade food? Write three sentences to explain why.

A special meal

WRITING A description

I can describe a special meal.

1 Have you ever tried food from another country? Work in groups. Make a list of dishes.

2 Read the blog. Which countries were Eduardo's dishes from?

New posts | About | Archives

Food adventures with Eduardo!

Our town has held an International Fair every year for the last four years. This summer's fair was the biggest we've ever had. Each class cooked tasty, traditional food from a different country. There were over 60 dishes from a dozen different countries, so I couldn't try everything!

I decided to try dishes from three countries. My starter was a small Japanese dish called sushi. This rice dish often contains raw fish, but I have a fish allergy, so I chose the colourful, vegetarian option. For the main course, I had spicy Mexican tamales with beans. Delicious! My dessert was a sweet Turkish dish called cezerye. It had nuts and carrots in it!

In my opinion, it wasn't the best meal I've ever eaten because it was an unusual mixture. However, it was a great way to try some international food.

3 Look at the **Useful language**. How do you say these expressions in your language?

Useful language
Describing a meal
I decided to try …
My starter / dessert was …
This (rice) dish contains …
For the main course I had a Turkish / Spanish / Mexican dish called …
In my opinion, it was delicious / amazing / the best meal I've ever had.
It was disappointing / terrible / the worst meal I've ever had.

4 Read the **Look!** box. Find examples of how Eduardo describes food in the text.

Look! Order of adjectives

You can use two adjectives together to make your writing interesting.
Adjectives usually follow this order:

opinion → **size / shape / colour** → **nationality / type / state**

opinion	size/shape/colour	nationality/type/state
sweet	small	traditional
tasty	round	Japanese
spicy	colourful	vegetarian
delicious	red	Mexican
plain		frozen
disgusting		

5 Copy and complete the sentences with the adjectives in the correct order.

   I ordered some rice.   boiled / plain
   I ordered some plain boiled rice.
1 I wanted a burger.   vegetarian / large
2 We had a curry.   Indian / delicious
3 They ordered some side dishes.   vegetarian / small
4 The dessert was yoghurt.   frozen / tasty
5 The waiter brought a menu.   big / green
6 Jo had peas with her fish and chips.   fresh / green
7 Each place had a napkin.   white / crisp

6 Write a blog post about a special meal. Follow the steps in the **Writing plan**.

Writing plan

Prepare
› Write notes about your special meal.
› Think about when and where you ate the meal.
› Where was it from?
› What were the dishes like?

Write
› Think of an interesting title for your blog post.
› Use adjectives to describe your courses and dishes.
› Summarize with your own thoughts and opinions.
› Use the expressions from the **Useful language** box.

Reflect
› Check your grammar: you can use an informal style with short forms.
› Check your spelling and order of adjectives.

W Writing summary: **WB** p. 86
R Review: Units 1–3 **SB** pp. 100–101
P Project: Units 1–3 **SB** pp. 106–107
L Literature: Units 1–3 **SB** pp. 112–113
E Exams: Unit 3 **SB** p. 120
LS Language summary: Unit 3 **SB** p. 129

Dream big

Vocabulary: Job sectors; Adjectives of personality
Grammar: Future forms; First conditional: *if* and *unless*; *might* vs *will* + adverbs
Speaking: Giving opinions
Writing: Future plans

VOCABULARY Jobs and job sectors

I can use compound nouns for jobs and to talk about job sectors.

1. In pairs, think of two interesting jobs. What makes these jobs interesting?

2. Use one word from each box to make jobs.

   A | care   music   sports   tour   web   wildlife

   B | designer   guide   instructor   photographer   tutor   worker

   tour guide

3. 🔊 **4.1** Match the jobs in Exercise 2 with the pictures 1–6. Listen and check.

4. In your notebook, number the job sectors in the box from 1 (your most favourite) to 11 (your least favourite).

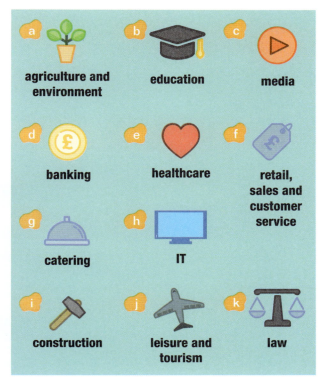

a agriculture and environment
b education
c media
d banking
e healthcare
f retail, sales and customer service
g catering
h IT
i construction
j leisure and tourism
k law

5. 🔊 **4.2** Listen to Sam discuss the survey with his mum. What are the three most popular and the three least popular job sectors?

6. Work in pairs. Discuss the questions.
   1. What job do you want to do?
   2. Which job sector is it in?

> **Look!** *in the ... industry*
>
> We can also say:
> *I'd like to work **in the** retail / banking / food **industry**.*

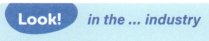
Now watch the vlog.

FAST FINISHER

Think of the people in your town. What job sectors do they work in? Make a list.

Language summary: Unit 4 SB p. 130

39

What happens when …?

READING **I can** understand pronoun references in a news article.

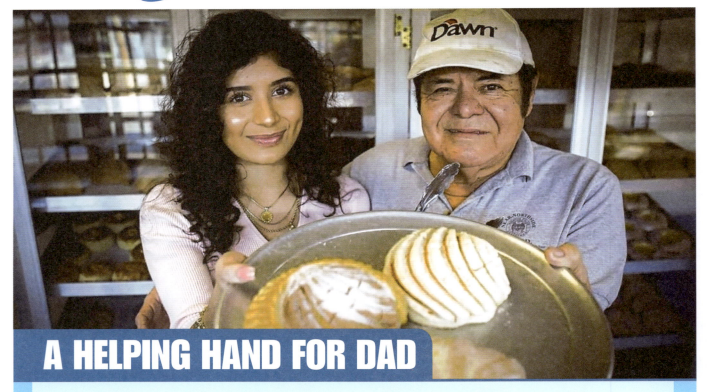

A HELPING HAND FOR DAD

You're still at school, but you've got plans for the future. Your family has a business and you're going to work in it. But what happens when the business gets into difficulty?

Jackie Garza's dad, Trinidad, has worked in the catering industry since he was a boy. He learned to make sweet and savoury bread rolls in his family's bakery in Mexico. Everybody loved them. After Trinidad moved to Houston, in the United States, he found an abandoned restaurant and turned it into La Casa, a bakery and café. But there weren't enough customers and he decided to close the café. However, he didn't realise that Jackie had a plan.

Jackie is passionate about the family business. She helps out at weekends and after school along with her three brothers. They all know that their dad makes amazing food, but Jackie wanted others to know about the café, too, so she posted a tweet. The tweet went viral and more than 60,000 people liked it. Customers came to try out Trinidad's baking, and comments came from Japan, Australia and Europe. Jackie was surprised by the reaction on social media. Thanks to this, she now feels confident about the future of the café. Things will definitely get better.

Jackie's dad admits he doesn't know how to use social media. He'll leave that to Jackie in the future. As well as studying, she'll probably be dealing with La Casa's social media accounts. She's also going to improve the website for the café. Will she take over the café one day? She wants to, but first she needs to finish high school. She's going to study business at university and learn skills that she can use in La Casa. It isn't going to be easy, but Jackie is determined.

1 🔊 **4.3** Listen and read the article. How did Jackie get more customers for her dad?

2 Read the article again. Copy and complete the sentences. Use three words in each gap.

Jackie's dad started working in *the catering industry* when he was a boy.
1 He set up the café after … the United States.
2 Trinidad decided to … because there weren't enough customers.
3 Jackie … to let others know about the café.
4 The reaction … made Jackie feel confident.
5 Jackie wants … she can use in La Casa.

3 Look at the blue pronouns in the text. What does each pronoun refer to?

it – the business

4 **Word Power** A *tweet* is a message sent on Twitter. *To tweet* is to send a message. With a partner, make a list of other social media nouns and verbs.

a comment, to comment …

5 💡 **GET CREATIVE** Do you know any family businesses? What are the advantages and disadvantages of working with your family? In small groups, make a presentation.

GRAMMAR Future forms

 I can use different tenses to talk about the future.

👁 Now watch the grammar animation.

1 Read the grammar box. Copy and complete the rules with the correct future form in your notebook.

---

be going to and will

Affirmative

I**'m going to study** business at university.
She**'s going to improve** the business.
Things **will definitely get** better.

Negative

It **isn't going to be** easy.
She **won't finish** school until she's 18.
They **probably won't close** the café.

Rules

We use [1]… for future intentions and predictions based on information or evidence.
We use [2]… for general predictions about the future.
We often use [3]… with the adverbs *possibly*, *probably* and *definitely* to express degrees of certainty.

---

2 Complete the article with the correct phrase from the box.

is going to return	isn't going to use
'll definitely give	'll probably do	're going to see
will … miss	won't want	won't lose

Robot shop assistant loses his job after only one week!

Robots are coming! According to some specialists we **'re going to see** more robots in offices, at airports, in hotels – in fact, in lots of different workplaces. They [1]… the more boring and repetitive jobs that humans don't enjoy. Fantastic news! However, shop owners and managers [2]… to employ a robot called Fabio.

He worked in a supermarket in Scotland. He met customers with a cheerful 'Hello!', but then he annoyed them by sending them in the wrong direction. Others found him scary. As a result, the supermarket [3]… him any more. Instead, it [4]… Fabio to the designers! Scientists say they [5]… him more training before they send him out to work again. [6]… anybody … him? A couple of his work colleagues were sad he had to leave. But at least they know they [7]… their jobs to a robot just yet!

---

3 PRONUNCIATION 'll

🔊 **4.4** Listen and repeat the contractions.

I'll You'll We'll She'll He'll They'll

4 🔊 **4.5** Listen and repeat the six phrases you hear. Do you hear *will* or the contraction *'ll*?

5 Complete the questions. Use *be going to* and *will*.

1 **A:** … (you / be) at home later?
  B: No, I'm working at the swimming pool until 9 p.m. I'm the new swimming instructor!
2 **A:** Where … (Jack / work) this summer?
  B: He's going to work in his uncle's shop.
3 **A:** … (the supermarket / definitely get) another robot?
  B: No, I don't think it will.
4 **A:** … (your new job / be) fun?
  B: It will probably be fun. And I'll get lots of free books!
5 **A:** Who … (work) in tourism?
  B: Sam is. He's going to be a tour guide.

6 Copy the grammar box and choose the correct answer to complete the rule.

Future continuous

+ She'll be dealing with the social media accounts.
− I won't be working late tonight.
? Will you be looking for a job this summer?

Rules

We use the future continuous for actions that will be in progress at [1] *a particular time / an unknown time* in the future.

---

7 Complete the sentences with the future continuous form of the verbs in brackets.

1 Don't call me before 7 p.m. I … (practise) for my singing exam.
2 My sister … (wait) for me when the bus arrives.
3 I … (not work) in my aunt's café this summer.
4 Jake … (not come) to the party. He … (look after) his little brother.
5 '… (your friend / do) more voluntary work next year?' 'Yes, she will.'

FUN FACT Experts predict that by 2035 robots will be doing 35% of the jobs that humans do now.

» **FAST FINISHER**

A robot is going to spend a day at your school next week. What jobs will it be doing? Write five sentences.

LS Language summary: Unit 4 SB p. 130

Right for the job

VOCABULARY and LISTENING Adjectives of personality

I can identify personal information in a podcast.

WHAT COLOUR ARE YOU?

FIERY RED
confident
brave
independent

SUNSHINE YELLOW
sociable
positive
creative

COOL BLUE
honest
sensible
curious

EARTH GREEN
patient
shy
calm

1 Look at the adjectives in the infographic. Match them with definitions 1–11 and write sentences in your notebook.

   A curious person always likes to know how things work.
   1 knows he/she can do something well
   2 is not angry when waiting or when something is difficult
   3 is relaxed and not often worried or excited
   4 has lots of original and unusual ideas
   5 makes good decisions
   6 doesn't show he/she is frightened
   7 enjoys being with people and meeting new people
   8 is happy and looks forward to the future
   9 is nervous or embarrassed when meeting people
   10 doesn't lie, cheat or steal
   11 can do things without the help of other people

2 Which adjectives describe you? What colour do you think you are? Discuss your answers in pairs.

3 Carrie Harris hopes to become an astronaut. Look at the picture. Decide which colour she is and which adjectives decribe her.

4 4.6 Listen to a podcast about Carrie. Which adjectives does the speaker use? Are they the same ones you chose?

5 4.6 Listen again. Are the sentences true (T) or false (F)? Correct the false sentences.
   1 Carrie has left school to start her space training.
   2 Carrie read a book about Mars six years ago.
   3 Carrie only wants to work in one job sector.
   4 NASA accepts a lot of young people on its space training programme.
   5 It's possible the temperature on Mars will be -60°C.
   6 Carrie is going to learn a new language.

6 FIND OUT What's the average temperature on Earth? How does this compare with Mars?

7 Work in pairs. Discuss the questions.
   1 Would you like to go into space? Why/Why not?
   2 Which other places would you like to explore?

LS Language summary: Unit 4 SB p. 130

GRAMMAR First conditional: *if* and *unless*; *might* vs *will* + adverbs

 use the first conditional for possible future events.

👁 Now watch the grammar animation.

1 Read the grammar box. Copy and complete examples 1–4 with the words in the box.

| might | 'll probably | will | won't |

First conditional

Situation	Result
If/Unless + present simple	*will/won't* + infinitive *might* + infinitive

If she gets a place on the programme, she [1] ... get a job as an astronaut.
Unless Carrie gets a place on the programme, she [2] ... get a job as an astronaut.
If she has to do another job, she [3] ... try something else in the space industry.
If she studies hard, she [4] ... learn Chinese very quickly.

Rules

We use the first conditional with *if* and *unless* to talk about possible future events and their results. We use *unless* to mean *if not*.
We use the adverbs *possibly* and *probably* and the modal verb *might* when the results are not certain.

Look! *if* clause + comma

When the situation (the *if* clause) is first, we use a comma after it. It is possible to show the result before the situation. In this case we remove the comma.
She'll learn Chinese very quickly if she studies hard.

2 Choose the correct answers.

1. She won't go to Mars *if / unless* she finishes the training.
2. Carrie's family will miss her *if / unless* she moves to Mars.
3. *If / Unless* she doesn't get a job in the space industry, she'll be unhappy.
4. The trip to Mars will be difficult *if / unless* the astronauts prepare for it.
5. *If / Unless* Carrie goes into space, she won't see her friends for a long time.
6. *If / Unless* Carrie learns different languages, she'll communicate better with other astronauts.

3 In your notebook, complete the sentences.

If your sister *gets* (get) a job in the café, I*'ll see* (see) her every day.
1. We ... (not say) anything about the party unless she ... (ask) about it.
2. My dad ... probably ... (be) angry, if I ... (arrive) home late.
3. If he ... (find) a summer job, he ... (might not come) on holiday with us.
4. If you ... (talk) to your teacher, you ... (feel) better.
5. If I ... (come) to your house later, ... (you/be) there?

4 🔊 4.7 Look at the picture and complete the text with the correct form of the verbs in the box. Listen and check.

| be | change | get | give | help | not like |

If Easton's idea works, it will change Momo's life.

Easton LaChappelle has always been curious about how things work. When he was a teenager, he made his first robotic arm with things he found at home. Easton has arranged to meet Momo and he's testing his robotic arm on her. If his design works, it *will give* Momo the chance to swim and paint – just like her friends. The pair get on really well and Easton loves the fact that Momo's very honest. If she [1] ... something, she'll probably tell him. If he gets the design right, the new arm [2] ... Momo's life.

However, robotic designs are very expensive, so Easton wants to make his robotic arms cheaper. But unless he [3] ... more money, his idea won't work. For that reason, he uses the internet to tell people about his design. If they like it, they [4] ... probably ... him.

Easton is confident about the future. He wants to donate 100 robotic arms to people who can't afford them. If he can change lives like Momo's, that [5] ... something to be proud of!

»» FAST FINISHER

Think about four of your friends or classmates. What job do you think they might do if they work/train hard?

 Language summary: Unit 4 SB p. 130

What next?

READING and LISTENING

I can pick out key information in an information leaflet.

Are you wondering what to do after you leave school? Why not combine your studies with some work experience on one of our apprenticeship courses?

A …
Are you curious about how things work? If so, you will love this course. First, you'll learn basic engineering skills and then do specialist training in an area that you enjoy. This could be in computer design, construction, transport or even aviation. This is a year-long course and you will work one day a week in a local company. There are a huge number of job opportunities for engineers. So, what are you waiting for?

B …
If you love sport and want to help others to get fit, this course will help you get the right skills. We deliver the programme together with the Fit4you gym. Half of your week will be in the gym with expert tutors and real customers. Numbers are limited for this one-year course, so don't wait too long to sign up.

C …
Do you want to see the world and meet people? The tourism industry is growing fast and needs people like you. On this two-year course, successful students will leave with the right skills to work as tour guides and travel agents. Some students go on to study hotel management. All students can choose to spend their final month working in a hotel here or abroad.

HIGH PEAK COLLEGE OPEN DAY!
Saturday 25 May

Gates open at 9 a.m. Guided tours of the college start at 11.30. To reserve your place, go to **www.highpeakcollege.org**
You need to book in advance.

What our students have said:

'I felt more confident after taking this course and I soon found a job as a tour guide.' Navid, 17

'I'm half-way through my computer design course. I'm very creative, so this course is perfect!' Liza, 18

1 Work in pairs. Look at the leaflet. Who is this information for?

2 Read the leaflet. Match a course in the box with the descriptions. There are two options you do not need.

> Engineering   Event Management
> Exercise and fitness   Healthcare
> Travel and tourism

3 Read the leaflet from High Peak College. Answer the questions.
1. What is an apprenticeship course?
2. Which courses offer work experience for part of the week?
3. Which is the longest course?
4. How can students get more information about the courses?
5. Who is still doing a High Peak College course?

4 4.8 Listen to Imogen talking to her friend, Nick. What is Imogen looking at?

5 4.8 Listen again and answer the questions.
1. Who are the courses for?
2. Where is the open day?
3. What might Imogen and Nick do if they arrive early?

> **Look!** Present tenses for future use
>
> We use the present simple to talk about timetables and scheduled events.
> It **starts** at 9 a.m.
> We use the present continuous for future arrangements.
> We**'re having** an open day on Saturday 25 May.

6 Work in pairs. Which of the courses at High Peak College would you like to go on? Why?

SPEAKING Giving opinions

I can give reasons to support my point of view.

1 🔊 **4.9** Listen and read. Who is going to work for a relative?

> **Sophie:** Hi, Liam. Are you going to go to university?
> **Liam:** I'm not sure. I might go to college. I'm quite keen on the idea because lots of college courses offer work experience.
> **Sophie:** What course do you want to do?
> **Liam:** Well, I reckon it's important to do something you really enjoy. That's why I want to do music or sound engineering.
> **Sophie:** I'm sure you're right. You might get a job in the music industry.
> **Liam:** That would be so cool. What about you?
> **Sophie:** To be honest, I have no idea. I need to think about it. That's the reason I'm doing work experience at my uncle's web design company this summer.
> **Liam:** You're really patient and calm. I think you'll be great in an office.

2 🔊 **4.9** Listen and read again. Answer the questions with *S* (Sophie) or *L* (Liam).
Who …
1 is interested in sound engineering?
2 is doing work experience this summer?
3 is patient and calm?

3 🔊 **4.10** Listen and repeat the **Useful language**.

Useful language

Giving opinions
I'm (not) sure.
I'm quite keen on the idea because …
I reckon …
That's why …
I'm (not) sure you're right.
To be honest, …
That's the reason …
I think …

4 🔊 **4.11** Copy and complete the dialogue with words from the **Useful language** box. Listen and check.

> **Emma:** Hi, Ryan. What are you doing this summer?
> **Ryan:** I'm not sure. I might go to a summer camp.
> **Emma:** Why do you want to do that?
> **Ryan:** Well, I'm [1]… on the idea [2]… it will be fun learning new things.
> **Emma:** I'm [3]… you're right. If you go, you'll probably make lots of friends.
> **Ryan:** That's true. To be [4]…, it's only for two weeks, so it won't be all summer.
> **Emma:** I reckon you'll love it. You're really sociable. You can do sports all day.
> **Ryan:** That's [5]… I want to do it!

5 Work in pairs. Prepare a new dialogue about activities for the summer. Follow the steps in the **Speaking plan**.

go to a summer camp   help around the house
look after a younger brother/sister
meet friends   work in a family business

Speaking plan

Prepare
› Choose an activity from the box.
› Make notes about why you chose this activity.
› Use phrases from the **Useful language** box.

Speak
› Practise your dialogue.
› Act out your dialogue without notes.
› Swap roles and change the choice of place in your dialogue.

Reflect
› Did you give your opinions?
› How can you improve next time?

● Now play *Keep moving!*

» **FAST FINISHER**
Write three sentences about your plans for the next school holiday.

LS Language summary: Unit 4 **SB** p. 130

REAL CULTURE!

Top teenage jobs

I can use information to develop my opinions.

TOP JOBS

The top five weekend jobs for school students in the UK!

1	Babysitting
2	Newspaper delivery
3	Dog walking
4	Car washing
5	Gardening

WEEKEND JOBS
A SNAPSHOT

Many teenagers in the United Kingdom like to have a weekend job or volunteer part-time. It's a chance to learn useful skills and earn some money.

But things are changing. Recent reports suggest that the number of school students in employment outside school hours is going down.

Only one in five school-age teens now have jobs. In 1996, 42% of teens were combining part-time work with school compared to a more recent figure of less than 20%. So, what's the reason? While some teens argue that they want to focus more on important exams, others say employers don't want to give jobs to teenagers these days.

If you're interested in finding a weekend job, you'll find all the information you need here.

7 a.m. – 7 p.m.

This is the time school students can start and finish work once they are fourteen. They can't start before 7 a.m. and they can't finish after 7 p.m. They also can't work for more than one hour before school or for more than two hours on a school day or a Sunday. On Saturdays or during holidays, fourteen-year-olds can work a maximum of five hours, but over-fifteens can work up to eight hours per day.

- School students can be employed in retail and office administration.
- They can deliver newspapers and leaflets and work in cafés and restaurants.
- They can babysit or help families with jobs around the house.

- School students can't work in: petrol stations, factories, cinemas, fairgrounds, restaurant kitchens or butchers.
- They also can't collect rubbish or work in telephone sales.

12
The total number of hours a teen employee can work per week during term-time.

4

1 **Look at the top five weekend jobs in the text. Answer the questions.**
   1 Have you done any of these jobs?
   2 Would you like to do any of these jobs outside school? Why/Why not?

2 🔊 **4.12 Read and listen to the text about weekend jobs and answer the questions.**
   1 What is the most popular weekend job for school students in the UK?
   2 Why are weekend jobs popular with teens in the UK?
   3 What percentage of teenagers have part-time jobs now?
   4 What is one reason fewer teens are taking Saturday jobs?
   5 What is the earliest time a fourteen-year-old can start work?
   6 How many hours can a teen work on a school day?

3 Joel is fourteen years old and he would like a part-time job. Look at the list of rules for teenagers in the UK. Are the sentences true (T) or false (F)? Correct the false sentences.

RULES FOR TEENAGERS LOOKING FOR WORK

1 You can deliver newspapers starting at 6.30 a.m.
2 You can deliver leaflets before school for up to one hour.
3 You can't work in a restaurant after school for one hour.
4 You can work for the afternoon in a café on Saturdays.
5 You can't work as a babysitter.
6 You can work at a cinema on Saturday afternoons.
7 You can't help out in a restaurant kitchen at the weekend.

4 💭 **THINK CRITICALLY** Work in pairs. Look at the list of places where school-age students can't work. Decide why they are not suitable.

5 **Word Power** What's the difference between *employment, employer, employee* and *to be employed*? Find the examples in the text. Do you know any other words in this word family?

6 🔊 **4.13 Listen and read what Chloe and Mario say about their weekend jobs. Answer the questions.**

> I enjoy working in a shop at the weekend and it's made me more sociable and patient. At first, I was nervous about asking my boss questions, but I learned quickly! I organize my time well so that I do my homework during the week. I also like earning money, so I can save. I need it. I don't get any pocket money from my parents. I don't want to work in a shop when I leave school. I want to study law and work with an environmental charity.

Chloe, 16

> I used to help my uncle in his café. It was difficult remembering things, especially when it was busy, but I learned to stay calm. I feel more positive now about the future. The experience has made me realise that I definitely won't work in catering! I'm going to go to college soon to study agriculture. Perhaps I'll be a farmer one day.

Mario, 17

1 How has Chloe's job changed her?
2 When does Chloe do her homework?
3 What is she going to do when she leaves school?
4 Who was Mario's employer?
5 What did Mario learn in his part-time job?
6 What does he want to do when he finishes school?

7 🌐 **COMPARE CULTURES** What jobs can school-age students do in your country? How are they different or similar to the jobs school students can do in the UK?

👁 Now watch the culture video.

⏩ **FAST FINISHER**
What's the perfect part-time job and why? Write five sentences.

47

Future plans

WRITING A letter

> I can write a letter about my future plans and predictions.

1 Read the advert and Gabriel's reply. Why does Gabriel suggest two job ideas for the future?

> Hi, I'm Max, the editor of *Teen Voice* and I'd love to hear from you. Tell me what type of person you are, what plans you have for next year and what you'd like to be doing in five years' time. The best reply will win a prize!

Dear Max,

My name's Gabriel and I'm fifteen. I'm very sociable and have lots of friends at school. I often wonder what I'll do in the future. I've got some interesting plans.

Next year, I'll definitely be at school. I guess I'll have lots of homework and exams, but I'm going to study hard. I hope I'll do well. I'm also good at sport and I plan to join a new basketball team. That will mean I'll have to train hard because some of the other schools have really good teams, but I suppose I'll make some new friends in the team.

I'm not sure what I'll be doing in five years' time. One day, I hope to be a professional basketball player! If that isn't possible, I'll probably study music because it's my favourite subject. When I'm older, I might be a music teacher. Most of all, I want to be successful and have fun.

Gabriel

2 Read the letter again and put the phrases in order. (1–3)
- a plans for five years' time
- b plans for next year
- c personal information

3 Which plans is Gabriel sure about? Which is he not sure about?

4 Look at the **Useful language** box. How do you say these expressions in your language?

> **Useful language**
>
> **Speculating about the future**
> I often wonder what …
> I guess …
> I suppose …
> I hope to / I hope I'll / we'll …

5 In your notebooks, complete the sentences using a phrase from the **Useful language** box.

Next year, I *suppose* I'll take the next judo exam.
1. After my exams, I … I'll have more time to do charity work.
2. In ten years' time, I … I'll work in the family business.
3. I … working in another country would be like.
4. When I'm eighteen, I … I'll learn to drive.
5. In the future, I … to have children.

6 Read the **Look!** box. Find examples in the letter.

> **Look!** Future time expressions
>
> When we talk about the future, we often start sentences with a time expression.
> Next year, …
> In five/ten years' time, …
> One day, …
> When I'm eighteen/older, …
> In the future, …

7 Write to *Teen Voice* about your plans. Follow the steps in the **Writing plan**.

> **Writing plan**
>
> **Prepare**
> › Write notes about your ideas.
> › Think about what sort of person you are.
> › What are your plans for next year / five years' time?
>
> **Write**
> › Put your ideas in the correct order.
> › Use the ideas in the **Useful language** and Look! boxes.
>
> **Reflect**
> › Check your grammar: the correct future tense / first conditional, *will* or *might*.
> › Check your use of time expressions.

W Writing summary: **WB** p. 87   **E** Exams: Unit 4 **SB** p. 121   **LS** Language summary: Unit 4 **SB** p. 130

48

Get the message? 5

Vocabulary: Communication verbs and nouns | **Grammar:** Second conditional; must/need to/have to/should/ought to | **Speaking:** Asking for and giving clarification | **Writing:** Advice forum

VOCABULARY Communication verbs

I can describe different ways people communicate.

1 🔊 **5.1 Look at the pictures. Match the verbs in the box with the pictures. Listen and check.**

| apologize | argue | complain | discuss | explain | gossip |
| interrupt | repeat | scream | shout | translate | whisper |

1 whisper

2 Choose the correct answers.
1. We *whisper / scream* when Dad is asleep.
2. We *complained / discussed* ideas for our holiday.
3. My brother *translated / shouted* a German message.
4. We often *repeat / interrupt* jokes from that TV show.
5. Dad *complained / translated* about the mess.
6. I *apologized / repeated* to my sister.
7. We always *explain / argue* about who will win the cup.
8. Has the teacher *gossiped / explained* the homework yet?

3 Work in pairs. Discuss the questions.
1. What have you argued about recently?
2. When did you last whisper to a friend? Why?
3. Which teacher gives the best explanations in your school? Why are they good at it?

👁 Now watch the vlog.

» FAST FINISHER

Write a few lines of dialogue containing two different ways of speaking.

LS Language summary: Unit 5 SB p. 131

How we communicate

READING

 understand details in a report.

Speaking without words

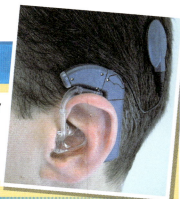

It's hard to believe, but over five per cent of the world's population can't hear very well. This means the world is a very different place for millions of people, and that they have to communicate in a very different way. Can we rely on modern technology to help them communicate, or would it be better if everybody learned sign language? This report looks at the experience of one person, Lloyd.

Lip-reading

Lloyd has never heard his parents say his name. He has been completely deaf from birth, so his first language is sign language. Lloyd attends the Mary Hare School for deaf pupils, but his teachers don't use sign language. They speak clearly and most pupils 'read' the teachers' lips. Lip-reading is hard work, but it prepares students for the real world.

Sign language

Between lessons, pupils use sign language, using special hand signals and facial expressions. You can't shout or whisper in sign language, but you can gossip and argue. But there are problems: different countries use different signs in their languages, and most hearing people don't understand sign language. How do deaf people communicate with hearing people? Well, if Lloyd wants to catch a train, he hands a note to the ticket seller.

Cochlear implants

Several months ago, Lloyd made a big decision. He wants a cochlear implant in his ear, a special gadget to help him hear. How would life be different if he had an implant? Well, Lloyd would be able to hear his name for the first time - something really important to his identity. Also, the implant would help Lloyd speak more clearly. Some pupils don't think cochlear implants are a good idea. They think it's important for hearing people to learn how to communicate with deaf people. They told Lloyd, 'If I were you, I wouldn't get an implant. Why don't more hearing people learn sign language?'

Learning to hear

Lloyd went ahead with the operation, and a hearing specialist switched on the implant. At first, Lloyd was disappointed. He could hear a few sounds, but couldn't understand them. The few months after the operation were difficult. One day, he recorded a sweet sound on his phone. He listened to it again and again, but didn't know what it was. 'I was shocked to discover that it was bird song,' Lloyd said, smiling. Finally, he was learning to hear.

1 Look at these statements about sign language and lip-reading. Are they true (T) or false (F)? Discuss your answers in pairs.
 1 You only use your hands to speak sign language.
 2 Different countries have different sign languages.

2 🔊 **5.2** Listen and read the report. Check your answers.

3 Answer the questions.
 1 How do most pupils at the Mary Hare School understand their teachers?
 2 How do they communicate with their school friends between lessons?
 3 How do cochlear implants help people?
 4 Why did some people tell Lloyd not to have the implants?
 5 What sound made Lloyd smile?

4 **Word Power** Which words in the box describe body language and which describe speech?

asking	eye contact	facial expressions
frowning	hand signals	shouting
speaking	telling	whispering

5 🔍 **FIND OUT** Learn how to say 'Hello. Nice to meet you,' in British Sign Language and in the sign language of your country.

FUN FACT In 1967, Dr Albert Mehrabien researched how people communicate. He reported that only 7% of communication is through spoken words, and 93% is through body language and tone of voice.

GRAMMAR
Second conditional

 I can use the second conditional to talk about unreal events.

👁 Now watch the grammar animation.

1 Read the grammar box. Copy and complete the sentences.

> would/wouldn't + infinitive   if + past simple

Second conditional	
Situation	**Result**
If + past simple	would/wouldn't + infinitive
If he **had** an implant, how **would** life be different?	
If I **were** you, I **wouldn't get** an implant.	
If he **lived** in Paris, he **would speak** French very well.	

Rules

We use the second conditional to talk about unreal or unlikely events and their consequences.

We can start the sentence with either the situation (*if*) or the result.

We use ¹... for the situation.

We use ²... for the result.

2 Copy and complete the sentences with the correct form of the the verb in brackets.
1. If I didn't have an exam tomorrow, I ... (go) to the cinema.
2. If we ... (not understand) the grammar, we'd ask our teacher to explain it again.
3. If they lived in the UK, they ... (speak) perfect English.
4. My brothers never fight, but if they ... (argue), I think the older one ... (win).
5. If I ... (be) you, I wouldn't gossip about your friend's problems.
6. What ... you ... (do) if I ... (tell) you a secret?
7. Joe ... (be) really disappointed if he ... (not pass) his exam.
8. Where ... you ... (go) on holiday if you ... (be) rich?

3 Complete the sentences with a phrase from the box.

> be/invited   buy/house   have/horse
> learn/sign language   visit/Mars

1. If I had a million euros, ...
2. If I had a spaceship, ...
3. I would learn to ride if I ... .
4. If my brother was deaf, ...
5. I would go to Phil's party if I ... .

4 🔊 5.3 Complete the text with the correct form of the words in brackets and the second conditional. Listen and check.

Communication matters: the interview

What *would* family life ¹... (be) like if one of your family ²... (be) deaf? We ask sisters Mia and Paula Allen.

Mia, you and your family have learned sign language. Why is that?

Well, the main reason we learned was to talk with my sister, Paula. We ³... (not / know) sign language if Paula ⁴... (not / be) deaf. Of course, if we ⁵... (not / use) sign language, she ⁶... (lip-read). But sign language helps us have a conversation together as a family.

Paula, would you like to attend a deaf school?

No, I don't think so because there aren't any near here. If I ⁷... (go) to a deaf school, I ⁸... (have to) live at the school. I don't want that. At the moment, I have a support teacher and my friends are learning to sign. They say it's quite easy and fun.

What are your future plans?

We would like to make online videos for families of deaf children. We're sure lots of people ⁹... (watch) if we ¹⁰... (have) our own channel.

> **Look!** *would* and *'d*
>
> When we speak, we often use the short form **'d** instead of **would** in affirmative sentences.

5 Write second conditional questions. In pairs, ask and answer.
1. what / you / do / if you / find / a mobile phone in the street?
2. if a friend / argue / with you / what / you / say?
3. you / learn / sign language / if a friend / teach you?
4. if you / win / a lot of money / what / you buy?
5. If / you / learn / a new skill / what / it / be?

> If I found a mobile phone in the street, I'd take it to the police station.

➤➤ **FAST FINISHER**

What videos would you and your friends make if you had an online video channel? Write five sentences.

 **Language summary: Unit 5 SB** p. 131

Express yourself

VOCABULARY and LISTENING Communication nouns

I can identify opinions.

10 awesome facts about language

1. Humans are great at *communication*. You probably say or write about 4,800 words a day!
2. There are about 7,000 languages in the world, so … between languages helps us to understand one another!
3. Sesquipedalophobia is a fear of long words! The … of this word is very difficult!
4. The word *set* has the most …s in the English language. It has over 400 meanings!
5. The … on your face changes the sound of your voice. Your listener can hear you smile on the phone.
6. The ancient Romans did not put spaces between words or use … marks like full stops.
7. What is the most popular topic for … on social media? It's technology and social media!
8. An … can be very annoying. If someone speaks when we are talking, we forget what what we've just said or heard.
9. Ancient Roman teachers used lots of … in their lessons. Science has proved that repeating things can help you to learn! But you have to do it many times.
10. Mandarin Chinese has 50,000 characters! My … is to learn the modern, simplified characters, not the traditional ones!

Traditional character: 飛
Simplified character: 飞

---

1 Read the text. Complete the sentences with the correct noun. There are two words you do not need.

> ~~communication~~   definition   description
> discussion   explanation   expression
> interruption   pronunciation   punctuation
> repetition   suggestion   translation

2 🔊 **5.4** Listen and check your answers. Work in pairs. Discuss which fact you found the most surprising.

3 Read the **Look!** box. Think of the verb for the other nouns in Exercise 1.

> **Look!** *-ion/-tion/-sion*
>
> We can use the endings *-ion/-tion/-sion* to change a verb into a noun.
> define – definition
> express – expression
> Often a spelling change is necessary.
> repeat – repetition

4 PRONUNCIATION Emphasis

> 🔊 **5.5** In these long words the stress falls on the second to last syllable. Listen and repeat the nouns from Exercise 1.
>
>
>
> communication   definition   description

5 🔊 **5.6** Listen to five dialogues. For each question, choose the correct answer.

1. You will hear a girl telling her friend about a school exchange trip to France. How did she feel about it?
   a Surprised that people didn't speak much English.
   b Sorry she didn't always know what the French family talked about.
   c Worried that the family didn't understand her.
2. You will hear two friends talking about a translation app. They both agree that the app …
   a included some useful phrases.
   b didn't help the boy write his essay.
   c was easy to find.
3. You will hear two friends talking about pronunciation. The boy advises his friend to …
   a read what is in his file.
   b do more practice tests.
   c practise saying words out loud.
4. You will hear a brother and sister arguing. They both agree …
   a it's better to study in different places.
   b they should switch the TV off.
   c they need to concentrate on revision.
5. You will hear two friends talking. What does Sara say is an important part of written communication?
   a good pronunciation
   b good writing skills
   c good punctuation

LS Language summary: Unit 5 SB p. 131

GRAMMAR Obligation: *must*; Necessity: *need to / have to*

 express obligation, necessity and advice.

👁 Now watch the grammar animation.

1 Read the grammar box. Look at the examples and find the infinitive in each sentence. Complete the rules.

Obligation: *must / mustn't* (+ infinitive)

I **must look** and see what the reviews are.
I **mustn't forget** to thank them.

Necessity: *need to / don't need to* (+ infinitive); *have to / don't have to* (+ infinitive)

I **need to practise** my pronunciation.
I **don't need to take** my PE kit to school tomorrow.
We've got a Maths test tomorrow, so I **have to study**.
I **don't have to wake up** early on Saturday morning.

Rules

We use ¹... when it is important to do something.
We use ²... when it's important NOT to do something.
We use ³... and ⁴... to talk about things that are necessary.
We use ⁵... and ⁶... to talk about things that are not necessary.

---

2 Read the text. Choose the correct answers.

BODY LANGUAGE clues

You ¹*mustn't / have to* understand someone's body language if you want to find out what mood they are in. If you want to understand the real meaning behind people's words, you ²*need to / mustn't* learn some body language signs. However, you don't ³*have to / mustn't* be an expert to work out if they are happy or sad.

People cross their arms in front of them when they don't want to communicate. If you want to look friendly, you ⁴*mustn't / don't have to* cross your arms.

Some people think you ⁵*need to / don't have to* look into the other person's eyes when you chat with them. They think that if someone doesn't look at you, it means they aren't telling the truth. However, this is not true. Some just feel more comfortable when they look away while you speak.

You ⁶*must / mustn't* forget about facial expressions, either. It isn't a good idea to roll your eyes when you are listening to others. It tells them you don't believe them or you feel bored!

3 Write affirmative or negative sentences so they are true for you. Use *must*, *need to* and *have to*. Use each verb at least once.

We / bring textbooks to our English class.
We must bring textbooks to our English class.
We don't have to bring textbooks to our English class.

1 We / speak English all the time.
2 We / do lots of pair work.
3 We / sit next to the same person every lesson.
4 We / be quiet when other people are talking.
5 We / revise for tests every lesson.

Advice: *should / ought to*

4 Read the grammar box. Complete the rules with *should*, *shouldn't* and *ought to*.

Advice: *should / shouldn't* (+ infinitive); *ought to / oughtn't to* (+ infinitive)

You **should repeat** the word a few times.
We **shouldn't study** late at night.
We **ought to turn** the television off now.

Rules

We use ¹... and ²... to give advice.
³... and *oughtn't to* have a similar meaning, but are less common.

---

5 Copy and complete the sentences with the affirmative or negative of the word in brackets.

1 You ... interrupt or shout in the lesson! (should)
2 Adam ... practise before his next piano lesson. (ought)
3 We ... discuss our plans for the weekend. (should)
4 They ... gossip so much about Joe. (should)
5 I ... work on my essay this evening. (ought)
6 The food's terrible. We ... complain! (ought)

6 Work in pairs. Give advice to a friend who is going to give a presentation to the class. Use *should / shouldn't* and *ought to / oughtn't to*.

smile / stay calm
not worry
look at the people you're speaking to
not cross your arms
make notes
listen carefully when people ask questions

You should smile and stay calm.

 FAST FINISHER

Write about two things you have to do this week and two things you should do to improve your English.

LS Language summary: Unit 5 **SB** p. 131

Do you really mean that?
READING and LISTENING

I can use facts and evaluate advice to form an opinion.

1 Read the *Advice Corner* on the web page. Work in pairs. Discuss which solutions (A–F) you would choose if you were Frankie.

Advice Corner   Home   About   Advice

This month we look at the issue of cyberbullying. What is it and what can we do about it?

This is an email from one of our followers, Frankie:

✉ New message

I've had a lot of messages that make me unhappy. They say bad things about me. Is it cyberbullying? What should I do?   *Frankie*

Possible solutions
A Reply with a rude message
B Explain that they should stop
C Tell a friend or family member
D Ignore the message
E Delete the message
F Something else

💡 Top *Tips!*

Here are our TOP TIPS to help people like Frankie deal with problem messages.

- First of all, you mustn't delete these messages – you may need to show someone the message.
- The next rule is you shouldn't reply – it only makes the situation worse.
- You should ignore the message, even if that's difficult.
- You must show an adult. They can help you.

2 Read the *Top Tips!* on the webpage. Are you still happy with your answer to Exercise 1? Discuss as a class.

3 🔊 5.7 Complete the *Fact File* with the words in the box to compare bullying and cyberbullying. Listen and check.

24 hours a day, 7 days a week	virtual
many people may see it	
people may not know the bully	verbal

Fact File: What is cyberbullying?

Bullying	Cyberbullying
• face-to-face	1 …
• may use words or actions	2 …
• the victim may be able to escape	3 …
• a few people may see it	4 …
• people know the bully	5 …

4 In pairs, explain the differences between bullying and cyberbullying. Why is cyberbullying often harder to deal with?

5 Read *Your story*. Would you use Trisha's app? Why/Why not?

YOUR STORY
TRISHA PRABHU
TEEN INVENTOR

When Trisha was thirteen, she read a lot about online bullying. She thought about designing an app to stop bullying – and help the bullies, too. Her research found that teenagers make quick decisions. They sometimes send hurtful messages without thinking.

Trisha invented an app called Re-Think. It works before you send a message, not after. When you write negative words it prompts you to think again. *Do you really mean that? Do you want to re-think?* Many users change their minds about their hurtful messages and don't send them. This helps the bullies as well as the people they are bullying.

6 💡 **GET CREATIVE** Create a poster to make people aware of the problems of cyberbullying. Include words and ideas from this page, and add pictures.

SPEAKING Asking for and giving clarification

I can ask for and give clarification.

1 🔊 **5.8 Listen and read. Why is Zac upset?**

Lena:	Hi, Zac. Can you hear me?
Zac:	Yeah. I got your message. What have I done? Can you explain?
Lena:	Huh? What do you mean? What message?
Zac:	You sent it yesterday evening. Hang on. I'll read it … 'Zac, you are so annoying.'
Lena:	Sorry, I didn't catch that. The signal here's not good. Can you repeat that?
Zac:	It said, 'Zac, you are so annoying.' I thought it was really rude.
Lena:	Oh no! I didn't mean that! I can explain … My phone is old and the screen is very small. I can't always see the letters. I meant to press *m* not *n*, but autocorrect changed the word. I'm so sorry I upset you. I feel awful now.
Zac:	Well, what was the message?
Lena:	'Zac, you are so amazing!'

2 Which of these problems do Lena and Zac have?
1 a bad connection
2 they've had an argument
3 they have to repeat themselves
4 one of them has been bullied
5 a small phone screen

3 🔊 **5.9 Listen and repeat the Useful language.**

Useful language

Asking for clarification
Can you explain?
What do/did you mean?
Sorry, I didn't catch that.
Can you repeat that?
Could you say that again?
What was that?
I'm not sure I understand.

Clarifying what you have said
I meant that/to …
I said that …
I didn't mean that.
I can explain.

4 🔊 **5.10 Copy and complete the dialogue with phrases from the Useful language box. Listen and check.**

George:	It's really noisy here again today, isn't it?
Ruby:	Yeah! They're doing more building work. We need to shout!
George:	¹… again? Sorry, I didn't ²… .
Ruby:	³… we need to shout!
George:	Yes, you're right. It's so boring!
Ruby:	Do you think I'm boring? I'm not sure ⁴… .
George:	I didn't ⁵… Don't be upset. I can ⁶… . I meant that the building work is boring, not you!

5 Work in pairs. Prepare your own dialogue. Choose one of these situations. Follow the steps in the Speaking plan.

| bad phone connection | noisy background |
| no signal / low battery | somebody is whispering |

Speaking plan

Prepare
› Choose a situation and decide who is asking for clarification.
› Make notes for your dialogue (what is the person asking for clarification about, how is it misunderstood?)

Speak
› Practise your dialogue.
› Use phrases from the **Useful language** box.
› Act out your dialogue without notes.
› Ask the class to identify your situation.

Reflect
› Did you use the expressions from the box?
› Did the class identify the situation?
› How can you improve next time?

👁 Now play *Keep moving!*

⟫ FAST FINISHER

Think of situations where people need to shout, repeat themselves or explain. Write a few lines of dialogue for one situation.

LS Language summary: Unit 5 SB p. 131

REAL CULTURE!

Not the only language
READING and LISTENING
I can identify opinions and explain them.

BRINGING LANGUAGES BACK TO LIFE

Although Great Britain and Ireland are English-speaking countries, did you know other languages are also spoken in these countries? In Ireland, around 10% of the population speaks Irish daily. In Wales, around 25% of people can speak Welsh, and around 30% of people in Scotland can speak Scots. Here, two young speakers of minority languages share their experiences.

Connemara, Ireland

I'm from Ireland and I go to a secondary school called a *Gaelscoil*. All our lessons are in Gaelic, or *Gaelighe*, the traditional language of Ireland. Irish people usually call this language Irish.

I'm bilingual, which is amazing, so I can translate things for my parents! They know some Gaelic, but they don't speak it and many Irish people have the same problem. They learned to read and write Gaelic at school, but everybody uses English, so they've forgotten it. You see Gaelic in road signs, but you don't hear it very often outside schools. Books, newspapers and TV programmes are usually in English, too. I think more TV channels ought to show Irish programmes like *Aifric*, a brilliant teen drama.

Around 1.7 million people here speak some Gaelic, while 82,000 people speak it daily outside schools. If more people went to a *Gaelscoil*, these numbers would grow. I believe that would be a positive thing because our language is part of our culture.

Slán (Goodbye!)

Caitlin (15)

I'm from Cornwall in England. It has sea on three sides, so it feels like a separate country. We even have our own flag and our own language! Cornish, or *Kernowek*, is the ancient language of Cornwall, but people stopped using it in the eighteenth century. Today, nobody speaks Cornish as their first language any more, although some people use it as their second language. Unfortunately, that number is small – these days, only 1% of people in Cornwall can speak Cornish.

However, the number of speakers is growing, especially among young people. Today, young children can learn the language at primary school and older people, like my parents, can take it at evening classes. Some of my friends have typical Cornish names, too, like *Demelza* and *Elowen* for girls or *Cadan* and *Santo* for boys. I think more young people should try Cornish so it doesn't die out, but I don't think everybody has to learn it. My pronunciation isn't great, but my friends and I like discussing stuff in a language other people don't understand. It's like a secret code!

Lowena dhis (Have a nice day!)

Jago (14)

Tintagel, Cornwall

The Cornish flag

1 ◉ 5.11 Read these phrases and guess the meaning. Listen and check. (Clue: they all mean the same thing in Irish, Welsh, Scots and Cornish.)

   Conas atá tú?   Sut wyt ti?
   Hoo are ye?   Fatla genes?

2 ◉ 5.12 Read and listen to the article. Which two languages do Caitlin and Jago tell us about?

3 Who talks about these things?
   Write C (Caitlin), J (Jago) or B (both).
   1 The way the media can help language learning.
   2 The difference between their parents' experience and their own.
   3 The role of schools in their language learning.
   4 The connection between culture and language.
   5 The fun of speaking a language other people don't understand.

4 ⊕ COMPARE CULTURES Work in pairs. Answer the questions.
   1 What languages are spoken in your country?
   2 Who speaks them and when and where do they use them?
   3 Which of them are the traditional languages of an area or region?

5 Find Jago's opinion of speaking Cornish and Caitlin's opinion of being bilingual. Explain each person's opinion and the reasons they give.

6 **Word Power** Work in pairs. Find languages ending in -ish in the article and add more -ish languages to your list. Other endings for language nouns include -ian and -ese. Add examples for these.

7 ◉ 5.13 Welsh is the only minority language with official status in the UK. What do you know about this language? Complete the Fact File with a word from the box. Listen and check.

   Argentina   Cymraeg   penguin
   town name   4,000   700,000

8 💬 THINK CRITICALLY In groups, discuss the questions.
   1 Should learning traditional languages be compulsory in schools?
   2 What are the benefits of language learning?
   3 Which languages are the most useful to know?

   ◉ Now watch the culture video.

   ≫ FAST FINISHER
   If you had the chance to study Mandarin Chinese, would you take it? Give reasons for your answer.

Fact File

1 The Welsh language is called … in Welsh. All UK passports contain English and Welsh.

2 There are over … native speakers of Welsh. That's around 20% of the population of Wales.

3 They think Welsh is one of the oldest languages in Europe. It's believed to be over … years old.

4 People speak Welsh in the UK and …! Over 5,000 people there speak Welsh as their first language.

5 Wales is home to the longest … in Europe. Llanfairpwllgwyngyllgogerychwyrndrobwllllantysiliogogogoch has 58 letters!

6 The English word … comes from the Welsh word *pen gwyn*. In Welsh, this means 'white head' – even though penguins have black heads!

If I were you …

WRITING Advice forum

I can give relevant advice with reasons in a forum.

1 Read the problem and the reply. Which part of Ben's advice do you think is most helpful?

Help! by Ollie14

I missed three weeks of school due to illness and now I have to revise for an English exam. I've watched lots of American comedy just because it's fun, but I can't remember important vocabulary and grammar. I'm worried as I've only got two days to revise. What should I do?

POST REPLY

BasketballBen

First of all, I'm sorry to hear about your problem. Too many people panic due to exam nerves. You should try to relax in order to focus better. When I'm revising, I do deep breathing exercises. They really help!

I also think you ought to listen to some English music. The reason is that you can listen to English in a relaxing way. Find songs that you like so that you play them lots of times. It's a good way to learn some really good English phrases.

If I were you, that's what I'd do. Good luck!

2 Work in pairs. Advise Ollie about his problem using the phrases in the box. Make notes and share with the class.

> get a friend to help you
> read and repeat words
> record notes and listen to them
> write sentences with the new grammar
> use a revision app

3 Look at the **Useful language**. How do you say these expressions in your language?

Useful language

Giving reasons

(just) because	as
due to (+ noun phrase)	that's why …
because of (+ noun phrase)	the reason is that …

NOTE: *as* and *due to* are a little more formal

4 Study the **Look!** box. Find two examples in Ben's reply.

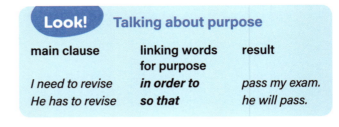

Look! Talking about purpose

main clause	linking words for purpose	result
I need to revise	**in order to**	pass my exam.
He has to revise	**so that**	he will pass.

5 In your notebooks, write the sentences in the correct order.

1 in order to / You should use an app / improve your grammar
2 Students ought to / repeat new words / they learn them well / so that
3 I should finish my homework quickly / I can go to the football match / so that
4 in order to / Please leave classrooms quickly / arrive at your next lesson on time
5 so that / I got up early / I could study before the exam.

6 Read Tara's problem. Write your advice. Follow the steps in the **Writing plan**.

Help! by TaraDancer

I have to learn some Portuguese because my cousins from Portugal are coming to stay. I've only got a week to learn some basic phrases. What should I do?

POST REPLY

Writing plan

Prepare
› With a partner, discuss ideas for advice.
› Choose the best two ideas to use.

Write
› Organize your ideas
  • name the problem and say you understand
  • say what you do
  • give your advice
  • send your best wishes
› Use the expressions from the **Useful language** box.

Reflect
› Check your grammar: second conditional (*If I were you …*); should/ought to/must/need to
› Check spelling of short forms and the position of apostrophes.

Teamwork

Vocabulary: Sports verbs; Adverbs of manner | **Grammar:** Relative pronouns; Indefinite pronouns; *can, could, be able to; be allowed to* | **Speaking:** Giving a group presentation | **Writing:** FAQs

VOCABULARY Sports verbs

I can use verbs for sports actions and events.

What do you know about SPORT?

If you don't know the answer, just guess!

1. In 2005, Australian David Schummy broke a record, when he *threw* an object 427.2 metres. What did he throw?
   a a baseball   b a frisbee   c a boomerang

2. The first time women *competed* in the Olympics was in Paris. What year was it?
   a 1900   b 1912   c 1924

3. Alyssa Healy broke a world record in 2019 when she *caught* a ball from a distance of 80 metres. What kind of ball was it?
   a a tennis ball   b a cricket ball   c a volley ball

4. The Denver Nuggets and Detroit Pistons set a record in 1983. Both teams *attacked* the goal and *scored* again and again. The final score was 186–184. What was the sport?
   a volleyball   b basketball   c dodgeball

5. In the first men's football World Cup in 1930, Uruguay *beat* … in the final.
   a Mexico   b Colombia   c Argentina

6. Usain Bolt *trained* hard and became the fastest person in the world. What was his secret?
   a eating well   b sleep   c practice

7. In 2019, over 290,000 official fans *supported* which club?
   a Manchester United   b Bayern Munich   c FC Barcelona

8. In the 2016 Olympics in Rio de Janeiro, Katie Ledecky successfully *defended* her Olympic title. What is her sport?
   a swimming
   b gymnastics
   c running

9. The opening ceremony for the first Paralympic Games was on 18 September 1960. Which country *organized* these Games?
   a Italy
   b Japan
   c Australia

10. In 2018, nearly 70,000 fans *attended* the Super Bowl. It was the final game of the season for which sport?
    a basketball
    b American football
    c baseball

---

1 🔊 6.1 Read and listen to the quiz. Write the answers in your notebook.

2 🔊 6.2 Listen and check your answers.

3 Read the quiz again. Write the infinitive of the blue verbs.

4 In pairs, match the verbs in Exercise 3 with expressions a–h to make collocations about sport.
   a a match or game
   b a football club
   c a goal or point
   d a ball (to another player)
   e the other team
   f for a race
   g a title
   h a ball (with one hand)

5 Work in pairs. Discuss which teams you support and which sports you do or watch. What is your best sporting memory?

   👁 Now watch the vlog.

▶▶ FAST FINISHER

Write three sentences about a sportsperson you know well using the verbs from Exercise 3.

LS Language summary: Unit 6 **SB** p. 132

59

Bringing a magical sport to life

READING **I can** work out the meaning of unknown words.

1. Look at the photo. What do you notice about the players?
2. 🔊 6.3 Read and listen to the interview. What do the blue words have in common?

Hoops and broomsticks

Today I'm meeting Kerry and Matt on the pitch where they play quidditch, to learn something about this unusual sport.

▶ **So, tell me about quidditch.**

Kerry: Originally, quidditch was a fictional sport from the *Harry Potter* series. In the books and films, the players flew on broomsticks. The game which we play is similar, and we do still use broomsticks, but of course nobody can fly!

Matt: It's like a mix of basketball, dodgeball, rugby and soccer. The first real-life games took place in the USA in 2005, but now there are teams almost everywhere. There's a World Cup, too.

▶ **Can you explain the basic rules?**

Kerry: Each team has seven players and the aim is to score points. Teams can get ten points by throwing balls through one of the three hoops which belong to the opposing team.

Matt: There are three types of ball and four different types of player. The first kind of ball is called a quaffle, and this is used to score points. The second type of ball is a bludger. Certain players can throw bludgers to try and hit members of the other team! The final type of ball is the most special and it's called the golden snitch. This is a tennis ball which is attached to the back of someone who is not in a team. When a player catches the golden snitch, their team gets 30 points and the game ends!

Kerry: That's right, and each player has a job to do. I'm a seeker, so it's my job to catch the golden snitch! Matt is a chaser – he's an attacker and scores by throwing the quaffle through the other team's hoops. Just like in football, we have keepers who defend the hoops. Finally, we also have beaters – these players try to hit the bludgers that the other team throw. Don't worry, it's not complicated once you start playing!

▶ **Why do you like it?**

Kerry: It's a fun, energetic sport. And the idea is a bit mad, which really appeals to young people.

Matt: And the club is really friendly. Anybody who loves competitive games can take part. Girls and boys play together, which is great.

▶ **Are there any bad points?**

Kerry: Some people don't think quidditch is a real sport, and that can be annoying.

Matt: That also means the fans that support us are usually just friends and family. We'd love more people to come along!

It looks like quidditch will take off as a sport. I can't wait to have a go!

3. Who says these things? Write *K* (Kerry) or *M* (Matt) and the word or phrase that tells you.
   1. Real-life quidditch is similar to the game in the books and films.
   2. Quidditch includes elements of other sports.
   3. Players have special roles within the teams.
   4. Young people find the game fun.
   5. It would be good to increase the number of fans.

4. Copy and complete the table with the blue words from the text.

Types of player (4)	Types of ball (3)	Other equipment (2)
seeker		

5. 💡 **GET CREATIVE** In pairs, choose another sport and write a short description. Don't say the name. Can the class guess what the sport is?

6. **Word Power** Find three phrasal verbs in the text. Match them with the correct meanings a–c.
   1. take off   a happen
   2. take place   b be involved in something
   3. take part   c grow or succeed

FUN FACT The Olympics has had mixed teams for some sports like equestrian (horse riding) events for many years. There are now new mixed-team events in table tennis, athletics and swimming. These include mixed-team relays and mixed doubles in table tennis.

6

GRAMMAR Relative pronouns; Indefinite pronouns

I can use relative pronouns and indefinite pronouns.

👁 Now watch the grammar animation.

1 Read the grammar box and copy the sentences. Write *people*, *things*, or *places* for each one.

> **Relative pronouns:** *who/that, which/that, where*
>
> They are on the pitch **where** they play quidditch.
> The game **which/that** we play is similar.
> The fans **who/that** support us are usually friends.
>
> **Rules**
> We use the relative pronouns:
> *which* or *that* to talk about ¹... .
> *who* or *that* to talk about ²... .
> *where* to talk about ³... .

2 Copy and complete the sentences with *who*, *which* or *where*. In which sentences could you use *that*?
1. The stadium ... we played last week was really big.
2. The balls ... we use are plastic.
3. The girl ... 's talking to Sam is his sister.
4. Amy and AJ are the players ... organize our team.
5. Here's the gym ... we practise sometimes.

3 Complete definitions 1–5. In pairs, make sentences with *who*, *which* or *where* and the words in the box.

> athlete   medal   member
> pitch   stadium   volleyball

a person ... takes part in competitive sports
An athlete is a person who takes part in competitive sports.

1. a green space ... teams play ball games
2. something ... you receive for winning a match
3. a sport ... two teams of six people play
4. somebody ... belongs to a team or club
5. a place ... supporters go to watch matches

4 Copy and complete the grammar box with the correct indefinite pronoun.

> **Indefinite pronouns**
> I'm meeting them to learn **something** about quidditch.
> Of course, **nobody** can fly!
> There are teams **everywhere**.

people	things	places
somebody	¹...	somewhere
²...	anything	anywhere
everybody	everything	³...
⁴...	nothing	nowhere

5 PRONUNCIATION Emphasis

🔊 **6.4** Listen and repeat the indefinite pronouns. Which syllable is stressed?

> anything   everybody   everywhere
> nothing   nowhere   somebody

6 Copy and complete the questions. Match the questions with the best answer.
1. Is there any... I can sit?
2. Can you ask some... to help us?
3. Is there any... I can do?
4. Have you got every... you need?
5. Has every... got their bags?
6. Is there any... at home?

a Yes. I'll get a shop assistant.
b No, but thanks for offering to help.
c Yes, there's a seat here.
d No, I've forgotten my phone.
e Yes, I think so. There's a light on.
f Yes, we've all got them.

7 Read the text and choose the correct answers. Do you agree with Tina and Nick's comments?

Better together?

¹**Everybody / Nobody** should have the chance to do sports. Boys and girls often play in different teams, but mixed teams are better. My volleyball team is mixed and we're top of the league! However, not ²**everybody / somebody** agrees.

Does ³**nothing / anything** need to change? What changes do you want to see in sports?

Comments

I agree. There should be more sportswomen on TV. Nearly ⁴**everything / nothing** you see on TV is about men in sport.   **TinaB**

In my opinion, if ⁵**nobody / somebody** enjoys a sport, that's good for their confidence.
⁶**Everybody / Nobody** should be able to choose the sport they want to play.   **Nick15**

8 In pairs, write three questions. Then ask the class.
Has anybody seen my pencil case? I can't find it.

» FAST FINISHER

Write definitions in English with *who/that*, *which/that* or *where* for three of these words.

> boomerang   medal winner   mixed team
> sports centre   sportswomen   supporter   team

A boomerang is a piece of wood which/that ...

LS Language summary: Unit 6 SB p. 132

61

Team building

VOCABULARY and LISTENING Adverbs of manner

I can understand the main points that different speakers make.

1 Look at the picture. Answer the questions.
1. Why do people do team-building tasks?
2. Would you like to do this? Why/Why not?

2 Read the **Look!** box. Copy and complete the rules using the words in the box.

| energetic – energetically   fast – fast   good – well |
| hard – hard   lazy – lazily   terrible – terribly |

Look!

We form regular adverbs by adding *-ly* to the adjective:
brilliant – brilliantly
For *-le* adjective endings, we drop the *-e*: ¹ …
For adjectives ending with *-ic*, we add *-ally*: ² …
For adjectives ending in *-y*, we change the *-y* to *-ily*: ³ …
Remember, some adjectives and adverbs are irregular: ⁴ …, ⁵ …, ⁶ …

3 🔊 6.5 You will hear people doing six team-building tasks. Choose the correct answers.
1. The team did the task *terribly / brilliantly*.
2. Seb crossed the river *badly / well*.
3. The class did the dance steps *lazily / energetically*.
4. Jess put the final brick on the tower *carefully / carelessly*.
5. Lily reacted to the problems *calmly / angrily*.
6. Jake climbed *nervously / confidently*.

4 Complete the sentences using the correct form of the word in brackets.

  Drive … (careful) here.
  Drive *carefully* here.
1. It's good for you to exercise … (regular).
2. My parents are … (happy) married.
3. Brush your teeth … (good).
4. They're playing music very … (loud).

5 🔊 6.6 Listen to Robbie, Martina and Carl. Which person is in the photo?

6 🔊 6.6 Listen again. For each question, choose the best answer.
1. Robbie's main problem was that …
   a. he didn't know how to give presentations.
   b. he didn't like speaking in front of groups.
   c. he couldn't breathe.
2. At the team-building day, Robbie learned …
   a. that some people knew more than him.
   b. that other people didn't listen to instructions.
   c. how to speak more confidently.
3. The team-building task helped Martina to …
   a. become a better leader.
   b. learn building skills.
   c. feel calm and patient.
4. In the 'plank-walk' exercise, Carl and his team members …
   a. practised confidently.
   b. worked well together.
   c. fell over a lot.

7 Work in pairs. Discuss how team-building tasks could help your class.

LS Language summary: Unit 6 **SB** p. 132

6

GRAMMAR Ability and permission:
can, could, be able to; be allowed to

I can use different forms of modals to talk about ability and permission.

◉ Now watch the grammar animation.

1 Read the grammar box. Copy and complete the rules with a phrase from the box.

| be able to | can/can't | could/couldn't |

Ability: can, could, be able to

Next time, I'**ll be able to** speak confidently.
I **couldn't** breathe.
I **can** listen to others now.
The team members **weren't able to** work well together.

Rules

We use the modal [1] ... (+ infinitive) to talk about present ability.
We use the modal [2] ... (+ infinitive) to talk about past ability.
We use the verb phrase [3] ... (+ infinitive) to talk about present, past or future ability.

2 Choose the correct answers.
1. *Were you able to / Can you* swim when you were five?
2. Ella *can't / couldn't* see the ball because the sun was in her eyes.
3. My grandmother *could / wasn't able to* run when she was 70 and she entered a half-marathon.
4. Look, Jon *can / could* ride that horse brilliantly!
5. I'd like to *can / be able to* make the basketball team next term.
6. *Can / Could* people watch sport online twenty years ago?

3 Complete the text with a phrase from the box.

| be able to | can (x2) | couldn't | wasn't able to |

🌐 HOME   ARTICLES   FAQs   🔍

A girl from Scotland who has autism and suffers from epilepsy has overcome her disabilities to win gold medals in skating. Murronrose Dunn won her first gold only fifteen months after starting lessons. Before she took it up, she thought she [1] ... skate because of her epilepsy, but it hasn't been a problem. She's a 'natural' on ice; she [2] ... skate brilliantly and she has won many competitions as a result.

It's helped her confidence. When she was young, Murronrose [3] ... make friends easily because of her autism. That has changed. Now, thanks to her success at skating, she [4] ... make new friends confidently. Will she [5] ... win more medals at her next competition? Maybe. She's certainly a name to watch.

4 Copy and complete the grammar box. Match the sentences with a rule, 1 or 2.

Permission: can/can't, be allowed to

You aren't [1] ... to touch the ground.
[2] ... I sit next to you?

Rules

1. We use the modal *can/can't* (+ infinitive) to ask for, give or refuse permission.
2. We use *be allowed to* or *can/can't* (+ infinitive) to talk about permission in general.

5 Complete the text with *can*, *can't* or *(not) allowed to*.

I love stand-up paddle boarding – or SUP for short! I'm [1] ... borrow my cousin's board, so I'm really lucky. I'm quite good at it now. The only problem is that I [2] ... only use it during the week because he goes paddle boarding every weekend.

I sometimes go with my brother Tom. He [3] ... use it without me now, because he used it a few months ago, but he was careless and left the board out in the sun. He [4] ... to use it when I'm with him! Maybe he [5] ... use it by himself when he's older and more responsible with other people's things.

6 In pairs, discuss what you can and can't do at home.

I can't stay out late.

⏭ **FAST FINISHER**

Do you have permission to borrow things from friends or family? Write two sentences about things you are/aren't allowed to borrow.

 Language summary: Unit 6 **SB** p. 132

63

KEEP TALKING!

Have a go!
READING and LISTENING

I can understand the most important information in a poster.

SUMMER FUN DAY! TAMARAMA BEACH 12 JANUARY

FOOTVOLLEY EXPERIENCE

This is a game which Brazilians play on the beach. It's a growing sport which mixes volleyball and football!

The 'pitch' is sand. Mixed teams are allowed. Four players in a team.

BOSSABALL EXPERIENCE

Join us to watch a game from Spain that mixes volleyball and gymnastics with samba music and a DJ!

The 'pitch' is a giant trampoline. Mixed teams are allowed. There are four or five players in a team.

FREE ENTRY

BRING YOUR FAMILY AND FRIENDS!
FIND OUT MORE
TAKE PART!

**CRAFT STALLS   DANCE SHOWS
DJ AND LIVE BANDS   FOOD STALLS
CLIMBING WALL   KITE COMPETITION**

STALLS OPEN   10.00 A.M. – 8.00 P.M.
EXHIBITION MATCHES AT   11.00 A.M.   12.00 P.M.   3.00 P.M.   4.00 P.M.

FOR MORE INFORMATION CONTACT: INFO@SUMMERFUN.AU OR FOLLOW US ON INSTAGRAM #SUMMERFUN

---

1 Read the poster above. Find and write the following information:
  1 the date the event takes place
  2 three sports you can try
  3 the time of the first exhibition match
  4 the time the event finishes

2 🔊 **6.7** Read the *Facts and rules*. Listen to a presentation about bossaball. Write the letter of the three facts you hear.

3 🔊 **6.8** Listen to a presentation about footvolley. Write the letter of the three facts you hear in the *Facts and rules*.

4 In pairs, discuss whether you would like to try these sports. Why/Why not?

5 **COMPARE CULTURES** Countries often have sports which are part of their culture. These are sometimes called national sports. What is your country's national sport? What other national sports do you know?

FACTS AND RULES
BOSSABALL OR FOOTVOLLEY?

A You aren't allowed to use your hands or arms.

B Players aren't allowed to touch the net.

C You score three points if you hit the playing area of the opposite team.

D You can only hit the ball once before passing it to another player.

E The first team to get fifteen points wins the game.

F You can get extra points for fancy gymnastic-style moves!

G Each team can touch the ball one, two or three times.

H You can't touch other players.

6

SPEAKING Giving a group presentation

I can prepare and give a presentation as part of a team.

1 🔊 **6.9** Listen and read. In pairs, answer the questions.
1. What is the activity Poppy and her team suggest?
2. Do you think this is a good suggestion for a fun day? Why/Why not?

Poppy: Good morning, everybody. I'm Poppy and I'd like to introduce Jamie and Ben. We're here to present an activity for the youth club Summer Fun Day – a scavenger hunt. It's fun and easy – anybody can do it. I'm going to hand over to Jamie, who will explain the details.

Jamie: First of all, I'll explain the basic rules. Each team has a list of things they must find or do. For example, you may need to find something like a sign on a building and take a selfie next to it. The winner is the team that finds everything in the shortest time. And now Ben will show you some pictures to give you a better idea.

Ben: A good scavenger hunt has a time limit. Teams usually have a list of ten or twelve tasks with clues. I'll show you some examples on the screen.

Poppy: We hope you like our suggestion. Thank you for listening. Are there any questions?

2 🔊 **6.10** Listen and repeat the **Useful language**.

Useful language

Introducing a presentation
I'd like to introduce …
We're here to present …
I'm going to hand over to Jamie, who …

Explaining your ideas
First of all, …
To start with, …
(Jamie) will explain (the details/rules).

Ending a presentation
We hope you like …
Thank you for listening.
Thank you for your time.

Inviting questions
Are there any questions?

3 🔊 **6.11** Complete Ella and Viktor's dialogue with the expressions in the box. Listen and check.

| like to introduce | for your time |
| have any questions | our idea | start with |

Ella and Viktor: Good afternoon, everybody.
Viktor: My name's Viktor and I'd ¹… Ella. We're here to present our suggestion for a Summer Fun Day activity. ²… is a talent show which anyone can participate in.
Ella: To ³…, I'll explain the idea. We need a team of three or four judges who will give each act a score out of ten. The act with the highest score wins.
Viktor: Thanks, Ella. And finally, does anybody ⁴…?
Ella: Please think carefully about our suggestion. Thank you ⁵… .

4 Work in small groups to make a team presentation. Choose an activity from the box. Follow the **Speaking plan**.

archery   a fancy dress race
a juggling demonstration   a treasure hunt

Speaking plan

Prepare
› Choose an activity.
› Make notes for your presentation.
› If possible, find pictures to illustrate your presentation.

Speak
› Decide who will give each part of the presentation.
› Use phrases from the **Useful language** box.
› Practise your presentation.
› Give your presentation and ask a classmate to listen or make a recording.
› Invite people to ask one or two questions and answer them.

Reflect
› Think about the questions people asked.
› What can you improve?

👁 Now play *Keep moving!*

›› FAST FINISHER

Choose one of the sports or activities from this unit. Write some facts and rules about it. Write questions for things you want to find out about it.

LS Language summary: Unit 6 **SB** p. 132

65

REAL CULTURE!

Who do you support?

I can use photos to find out information about a text.

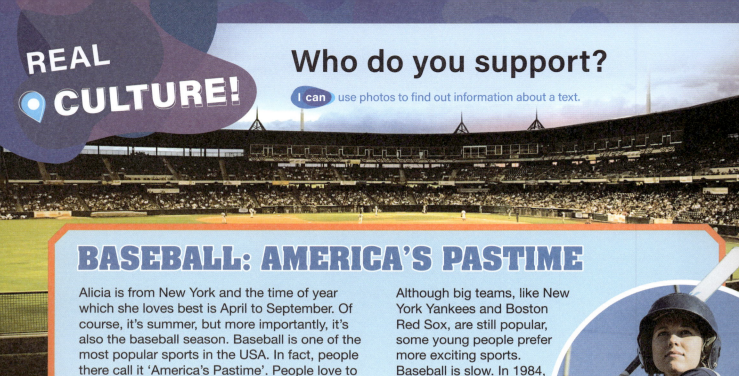

BASEBALL: AMERICA'S PASTIME

Alicia is from New York and the time of year which she loves best is April to September. Of course, it's summer, but more importantly, it's also the baseball season. Baseball is one of the most popular sports in the USA. In fact, people there call it 'America's Pastime'. People love to play it and watch it. The supporters who go to live events are allowed to take picnics to their local baseball ground, so it's a popular day out for families.

Although big teams, like New York Yankees and Boston Red Sox, are still popular, some young people prefer more exciting sports. Baseball is slow. In 1984, one game finished two days after it started! Alicia is a big Yankees supporter, but she also plays softball. Although it's a similar game, some young people prefer it because it's safer – the ball isn't as hard – and the field is smaller, so the game is faster.

> **Alicia says,**
> 'Our family used to go to games on summer evenings, even when I was a baby. I loved the sound of a bat hitting a ball and the friendly atmosphere in the stadium.'

AMERICAN FOOTBALL: TIME TO CHEER!

With fun team names like Dallas Cowboys and Miami Dolphins, American football attracts millions of spectators. It's fast and dangerous, so players wear helmets and shoulder pads.

The American football season begins in September and has some of its biggest matches during Thanksgiving and Christmas time. The final match of the season is the Super Bowl in early February. Over 100 million fans watch the match on TV and the half-time event has famous entertainers from the music industry. To many Americans, this day feels like a national holiday.

Before and during matches there are teams of people who shout, dance and perform next to the pitch. They are called cheerleaders and their job is to encourage the players and the supporters for their team. Cheerleading began in 1898 and the performers were originally all men. Adam, a cheerleader from Florida, gets mad with anybody who thinks cheerleading isn't a sport.

> **Adam says,**
> 'To be able to cheerlead well, you have to train hard. A lot of people think waving pom-poms looks easy, but I'm a gymnast and cheerleaders can train in the gym for two hours a day.'

There are four million cheerleaders in the USA!

American football is the number one sport in the USA. Baseball is number two.

6

1 Look at the pictures. Work in pairs and discuss what you know about these sports.

2 🔊 6.12 Student A: read and listen to the text *America's pastime*. Ask Student B questions 1–5 about American football.
   1 What do the players wear?
   2 When does the football season start?
   3 What is the final called?
   4 What is the name of the people who do a dance routine before the game?
   5 Why do they do this routine?

   🔊 6.13 Student B: read and listen to the text *Time to cheer*. Ask Student A questions 6–10 about baseball.
   6 When does the baseball season start?
   7 What are people allowed to take to matches?
   8 What sound did Alicia like when she was a child?
   9 Which teams are still popular?
   10 Why do some people prefer softball?

3 🔊 6.14 Listen to the dialogue. Complete the rules for each sport with the words in the box.

batter	catches	contact	defend (x2)
eleven	end zone	home run	nine
pitcher	point	score	six	touchdown

4 Work in pairs. Discuss which sport you would like to play and explain why.

5 **Word Power** Find examples of different sports places, people and equipment in the texts. Copy and complete the table.

place	person/sportsperson	equipment
ground	supporter	bat

6 🔍 **FIND OUT** What other sports are popular in the USA?

7 💬 **THINK CRITICALLY** In your country, what events bring people together? Why do you think people identify so strongly with particular sports and teams?

👁 Now watch the culture video.

⏩ **FAST FINISHER**
An American friend wants to go to a sports event in your country. Recommend an event and give reasons.

THE RULES

BASEBALL

- There are ¹… players in a team.
- The ²… throws the ball and the ³… hits the ball.
- There are four bases. Fielders from the other team ⁴… the bases.
- Batters run to the next base each time a player hits the ball. Each batter who passes all four bases scores a ⁵….
- If you hit the ball so hard you can run round all four bases in one go, you score a ⁶….
- Players are out if a fielder ⁷… the ball.

AMERICAN FOOTBALL

- There are ⁸… players in a team.
- American football is a ⁹… sport.
- The team can carry or kick the ball down the pitch towards their opponents' ¹⁰….
- Teams must ¹¹… their end zones.
- When a player gets the ball into the end zone the team scores ¹²… points – this is called a ¹³….
- Teams must ¹⁴… as many touchdowns as they can before the time is up.

67

What can we do?

WRITING FAQs

I can write clear, useful information for a particular audience.

1 Read the heading and the questions. Choose the correct meaning of *FAQs*. Who is this information for?

- Facts and Questions
- Frequently Asked Questions
- Fun and Quizzes

2 Read the information. In your opinion, which questions are most useful?

COSMIC BOWLING ALLEY FAQs

Where is Cosmic Bowling?
153 Harbour Lane, Middleton, NM5 ER2

How much is it?
ADULT one game – £5.75   CHILD one game – £4.25

Are there any special offers?
We have a group deal at the weekend. Four adult players for one game only £20.00, or two games for £32.00.
You can add extra players for only £4.00 a game!

What are your opening hours?
Sun – Thur: 10 a.m. – 11 p.m.
Fri and Sat: 10 a.m. – midnight.

Am I allowed to wear my own shoes?
No, you aren't allowed to wear your own shoes in the bowling area. You must collect special bowling shoes at the front desk.

Can I have a party at Cosmic?
Yes! It's a really amazing place for a birthday celebration or any other special occasion. Book early – we can get extremely busy!

Can we bring our own food and drink?
You aren't allowed to bring your own food and drink. Our café is quite big and there's a very good choice of snacks. Anybody who has a bowling ticket gets 10% off.

I have a different question. How can I contact you?
Email us: info@cosmic.com or call 01632 960235.

3 Look at the **Useful language** box. Are FAQs usually long or short?

Useful language
Using questions as headings
Where is it?   What are your opening hours?
How much is it?   Can I / we …?

4 Read the **Look!** box. Find examples in the FAQs. What is the difference between *very* and *really*?

Look! Making adjectives stronger or weaker

weaker ←——————————→ stronger
not very   quite   very   really   extremely

We usually use these words before an adjective.
Very and *really* have similar meanings. Remember:
We don't use *very* before a strong adjective.
~~very amazing~~ ✗
We use *really* before a strong adjective.
really amazing ✓

5 In your notebooks, copy and complete the pairs of sentences. Use the **Look!** box to help you.
1 I didn't like the food. = It *was very / wasn't very* tasty.
2 The price wasn't bad. = It was *quite / very* good.
3 We had to wait two hours to get in. = It was *extremely / quite* busy.
4 I enjoyed that a lot! = It was *very / really* amazing!

6 Write FAQs for visitors. Follow the steps in the **Writing plan**.

Writing plan

Prepare
> Choose a fun activity in your area for your school, neighbourhood, sports team or town.
> Research the prices, opening hours and other useful facts.

Write
> Write your FAQs and clear answers.
> Use question headings from the **Useful language** box.
> Use words from the Look! box to make adjectives stronger or weaker.

Reflect
> Check your grammar for *can / be able to / be allowed to*.
> Think about the person who will read this. Is your information clear, correct and helpful?

W Writing summary: **WB** p. 89
R Review: **Units 4–6 SB** pp. 102–103
P Project: **Units 4–6 SB** pp. 108–109
L Literature: **Units 4–6 SB** pp. 114–115
E Exams: **Unit 6 SB** p. 123
LS Language summary: **Unit 6 SB** p. 132

Rainbow Earth 7

Vocabulary: The natural environment; Environment verbs | **Grammar:** Present simple passive; Past simple passive | **Speaking:** Agreeing and disagreeing | **Writing:** A 'for and against' essay

VOCABULARY The natural environment

I can understand descriptions of the natural environment.

1 Look at the pictures and answer the questions.
1. What can you see in the pictures?
2. Where do you think these places are?

2 🔊 7.1 Read and listen to the words in boxes A–C.

A ~~cave(s)~~ coast cliff sand wave(s)
B glacier ice rock valley
C sunlight sunrise sunset

3 🔊 7.2 In your notebooks, complete the text with the correct words from each box. Listen and check.

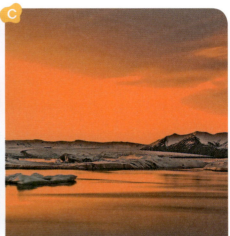

A The Purple Cathedral is one of the largest *caves* on the ¹… of New Zealand's South Island and is over 400 metres long. These cold, dark places form when powerful ocean ²… repeatedly hit the soft rock of a ³… . The waves pick up small stones and ⁴… from the beach. This causes erosion, which makes the cave bigger. But why is this landform purple? The colour purple comes from the red algae that covers the walls!

B A river that flows down a mountain creates a ⁵… . When the water freezes, it forms a ⁶… . These large areas of ⁷… move slowly down the mountain. They carry small stones and larger pieces of ⁸… with them. These erode the ground below, and over time make the valley bigger. The ice often looks blue because of the way it reflects light. Some glaciers around the world are melting because of climate change.

C It isn't always easy to sleep in Iceland! Thanks to the midnight sun, Iceland sometimes gets around twenty hours of ⁹… during the summer months! However, in winter, the days are short. You might wake up to a beautiful orange ¹⁰… at around 11 a.m. You have to be quick to enjoy the day, because ¹¹… occurs between 3 and 4 p.m.

4 In your notebooks, match 1–6 with a–f to make sentences.
1. I can't walk along the top of that   *1 c*
2. In summer, I love going
3. We took a boat along the
4. I wanted to stay up late to see the
5. When he came out of the cinema, the
6. The waves were noisy when they crashed

a. coast and stopped at a beach for lunch.
b. bright sunlight hurt his eyes.
c. cliff. It's too high and I hate heights!
d. against the rocks.
e. inside caves because they're always cool.
f. sunset. It's beautiful at this time of year.

5 Work in pairs. Which of the places in the text would you like to visit? Why?

6 🔍 **FIND OUT** What is the largest glacier in the world? Where is it and how big is it?

Now watch the vlog.

» FAST FINISHER
Write three sentences about the natural environment where you live.

Language summary: Unit 7 SB p. 133

69

Nature in brilliant blue!

READING   I can scan texts to find a main idea.

1 Look at the pictures. What else in the natural world is blue?

2 🔊 7.3 Scan the online article. Match headings 1–4 with paragraphs A–D. Listen and check.

1 Small, but deadly   2 A taste of blue   3 Why colour became important   4 Fantastic feet

Life in blue

🌿 iNature   HOME   ARTICLES   SUBMIT

A ...

Until 600 million years ago, colour wasn't important to the creatures on Earth – none of them had eyes! But as they started to develop sight, colours started to matter. Bright red or yellow creatures were dangerously visible to other hungry animals, while green creatures could safely hide amongst leaves and trees. But what about blue? From the sky to the sea, blue is all around us, but is it found in plants or animals?

B ...

Some animals appear blue because of their feathers, scales or shells, or because they eat certain foods. The blue-footed booby is found on the coast of Central and South America. Its blue feet are produced by pigments, or coloured chemicals, in the fish that they eat. Young and healthy birds have very bright blue feet, but the blue colour fades with age. When a female bird is looking for a partner, she looks for the one with the bluest feet.

C ...

Be very careful! Blue poison dart frogs aren't seen very easily. They are often hidden by leaves, sticks and rocks in the rainforest of Central and South America. They are only 1 cm long, so difficult for us to see, but they have excellent eyesight. Just touching one of them can be fatal. How can you avoid this? Head for the water. These tiny frogs haven't got webbed feet and are terrible swimmers!

D ...

Look at a $50 note from New Zealand and you might notice a pair of blue milk mushrooms. Can they be eaten? Yes, but they aren't very popular. The rarer the colour, the less popular it is on your plate! Blue is often added to foods such as sweets, but it's rarely found in nature, so it is made artificially. However, scientists in the food industry are excited about these mushrooms. Blue milk mushrooms might offer a natural alternative.

3 🔊 7.3 Read and listen to the article again. Choose the correct answer.

1 Colours became important for creatures when they started ...
   a hunting for food.
   b looking for partners.
   c seeing things clearly.

2 A booby's feet give information about ...
   a whether it wants a partner.
   b how old it is.
   c what it's just eaten.

3 Blue poison dart frogs ...
   a are difficult to see.
   b can swim well.
   c hide in water.

4 Blue milk mushrooms ...
   a are exciting to eat.
   b have a sweet taste.
   c can add colour to food.

4 **Word Power** Find the words connected to parts of animals and plants in the text. Use a dictionary to check their meanings.

5 **GET CREATIVE** In small groups, choose something with an unusual colour in the natural world. Find out why it is that colour. Share your information with the class.

FUN FACT Not all bees are black and yellow. Some sweat bees are a blue, green or brown colour.

7

GRAMMAR Present simple passive

I can use the present simple passive.

Now watch the grammar animation.

1 Copy and complete the grammar box with the correct present simple passive forms.

> aren't seen   is ... added   is ... found   they are

Affirmative	Negative
Its blue feet **are produced** by pigments in fish.	It **isn't found** in nature.
Blue [1] ... often ... to some foods.	The frogs [2] ... very easily.
Questions	**Short answers**
[3] ... it ... in plants or animals?	Yes, it **is**. / No, it **isn't**.
Are the colours **made** naturally?	Yes, [4] ... / No, they **aren't**.

Rules

We form the passive with the present simple of the verb *be* and the past participle.

2 Write the past simple and the past participle of the verbs.

> catch   carry   do   give   learn   make   post   say
> see   send   spend   study   take   use   watch

3 In your notebook, complete the sentences in the quiz with *is* or *are*. Then choose the correct answers.

fascinating facts!
Did you know ...?

1. Sunsets *are* seen by astronauts on the Space Station every *30 / 90* minutes in space.
2. Sand ... used to make *glass / paper*.
3. Fewer than *10 / 100* people per year ... attacked by sharks.
4. Ice ... formed when the temperature falls to *0°C / -10°C*.
5. Each year, two billion flowers ... grown in *Spain / the Netherlands* to sell in shops around the world.
6. Each year *605,000 / 65,000* tonnes of chocolate ... eaten in the UK.

4 Answer the questions.

> Are you taken to school by car? ✗
> *No, I'm not.*

1. Are they given milk at school? ✓
2. Is plastic made in factories? ✓
3. Is he asked to help make dinner? ✗
4. Are the emails sent each day? ✓
5. Are the students asked to write reports? ✗

5 🔊 7.4 Complete the article with the present simple passive of the verb in brackets. Listen and check.

DRONE PHOTOGRAPHY GETS THE PERFECT PICTURE!

What do you think was used to take this picture of a polar bear? Clue: This animal wasn't photographed by someone behind a camera.

Who doesn't like close-up photos of wild animals? A lot [1] ... (learn) about their behaviour from these pictures. Some photos [2] ... (take) on the ground, but other images [3] ... (capture) from the air above. In more remote areas, for example, helicopters [4] ... (often/use) because they can cover a larger area. Important information about the movement of wild animals [5] ... (collect) in this way. However, helicopters are noisy. Although some animals don't mind loud noises, others [6] ... (scare) by them. Drones can offer a cheaper, quieter alternative. The best images [7] ... (create) when animals are relaxed. You can see that for this bear, it was the right solution!

6 In pairs, make questions using the present simple passive. Take turns to ask and answer them.

1. Where / lots of shoes / make / ?
2. What wild animals / find / in Spain?
3. What things / sell / in the local market?
4. What animals / keep / as pets?
5. What / things / not allow / in your school?

» FAST FINISHER

Write about two other things that drone cameras are used for.

LS Language summary: Unit 7 **SB** p. 133

It's important ...

VOCABULARY and LISTENING
Environment verbs

I can use questions to predict what information to listen for.

1 🔊 **7.5** Listen and read. How do you say these verbs in your language?

1 clean up

2 collect

3 destroy

4 poison

5 pollute

6 protect

7 recycle

8 reuse

9 save

10 throw away

11 waste

2 In pairs, choose the correct answers.
1 We can *waste / save* water by having short showers.
2 Fires can *destroy / protect* large areas of forest.
3 Chemicals *clean up / poison* fish in rivers.
4 Cars and buses *pollute / protect* the air.
5 You shouldn't *throw away / save* plastic on the beach because it harms sea life.
6 You should *destroy / recycle* bottles and cans.
7 Children often *collect / waste* plastic animals.

3 Complete the text with the correct verb. The first letter is given.

When I was younger, I loved to c*ollect* plastic toys. I had hundreds. When I was a teenager, I read how these small plastic pieces [1] p... the ocean and [2] p... animals who think they're food. So, I didn't [3] t... the plastic toys. At first, I wanted to [4] r... them, but then I decided to use them to send a message about waste. I made a model in my art class to show how waste of all types [5] d... the environment. I think art is a great way to show people the problem and encourage them to [6] p... our planet.

4 Look at the statements in Exercise 5. What sort of information do you need to listen for?

1 I'm listening for a date and an event.

5 🔊 **7.6** Listen to Luke and Anna on the radio. Are the sentences are true (T) or false (F)? Correct the false sentences. Listen again and check.
1 World Environment day is 15th July.
2 Luke's friends organized an event.
3 Luke was annoyed when he saw rubbish in the sea.
4 Around 80 people helped Luke on the beach.
5 Rubbish is carried into the sea by wind.
6 Luke plans to clean up the beach every week.

6 In pairs, imagine you and your friends decide to clean up an area. Where is it? What sort of rubbish is there?

LS Language summary: Unit 7 **SB** p. 133

72

GRAMMAR Past simple passive

I can use the past simple passive.

◉ Now watch the grammar animation.

1 Copy and complete the grammar box with the correct past simple form of the verb *be*.

Affirmative	Negative
It ¹… liked by more than 80 people.	It (plastic) ²… seen as a problem.
Some tiny pieces of plastic ³… found on the rocks.	The smaller items ⁴… collected.
Questions	**Short answers**
⁵… all the rubbish collected?	Yes, it was. / No, it ⁶… .

Rules

We form the past simple passive with the past simple of the verb *be* and the past participle.

2 Copy and complete the sentences with *was/were*, *wasn't/weren't* and the verb in brackets.

Large areas of forest *were destroyed* by fire.
1 The 30 metre wave … (not see) until the last minute.
2 A bag that contained $2,000 … (find) in a cave.
3 Tiny insects … (discover) under an ancient glacier.
4 Plastic … (invent) in 1907, but plastic products … (not use) much until the 1960s.
5 A turtle … (rescue) after it had eaten a balloon.

3 Copy the dialogues. Write questions and short answers.

Were ¹… (you / send) an invitation to the event at the park?

Yes, I ²… . I got it last week.

³… (the event / organize) by your school?

No, it ⁴… . It was arranged by some students.

⁵… (prizes / give) for the best poster?

Yes, they ⁶… . My friend won one.

4 PRONUNCIATION Weak forms /wəz/ /wə/ or strong forms /wɒz/ /wɜː/

🔊 **7.7** Listen to the sentences. How do you say the underlined words? Listen and repeat.

<u>Was</u> it found on the beach? Yes, it <u>was</u>.
<u>Were</u> they seen near the cave? Yes, they <u>were</u>.

5 Complete the news story with the correct past simple passive form of the verb in brackets.

POLICE RESCUE BABY SQUIRREL!

An emergency call *was received* (receive) by the police in Karlsruhe, Germany. The caller sounded very scared. Police officers ¹… quickly … (send) to the scene of the crime. When they found the man, he told them that a baby squirrel was chasing him. Police believe the squirrel was probably looking for its mother. ²… it … (catch)? Yes, it ³… . The drama ended when the tiny squirrel ⁴… (discover) nearby. But it was so tired it had fallen asleep! As it's important to protect squirrels, it ⁵… (take) to the police station, but it ⁶… (not keep) there for long. It ⁷… (collect) by volunteers from a local animal rescue centre.

6 Copy the grammar box. Complete the information with the labels: *active* and *passive*.

	[agent]	[object]
1 …	The police received	an emergency call.
	[subject]	[agent]
2 …	An emergency call	was received by the police.

Rules

The object of an active sentence becomes the subject of a passive sentence.

7 Rewrite the sentences in the past simple passive.
1 They didn't throw away the party food.
2 The students cleaned up the park at the weekend.
3 The strong wind didn't destroy the trees.
4 Did the school reuse the old textbooks?
5 The group collected the rubbish.

8 In pairs, write three sentences about some recent news using the past simple passive.

A festival was held in the local park.

» FAST FINISHER

Write three true and three false sentences in the past simple passive. Use these verbs or your own ideas.

| give | invite | catch | find | steal | collect |

We were given a lot of homework yesterday!

LS Language summary: Unit 7 **SB** p. 133

KEEP TALKING!

Plastic free!
READING and LISTENING

I can understand facts and figures in an infographic.

1 Read the infographic quickly. Which is the biggest number you can see? What does it refer to?

WHAT A WASTE!
SAY NO TO PLASTIC STRAWS!

Plastic straws come in all sorts of crazy colours. Some bend and some change colour when you're drinking. They might be fun at parties, but straws are causing huge problems for the environment.

HISTORY OF STRAWS

Drinking straws are not a new invention. In ancient Egypt, straws were often used to stop people drinking insects that had fallen into their cups. The first straws were made of gold and wheat and then paper. It was believed that they were hygienic, as glasses and cups could be dirty. From the 1960s onwards, takeaway food and drinks became more popular and the plastic straw became common.

10 One plastic straw is made in ten minutes, but it stays on the Earth forever. Straws are light, so the wind carries them easily. They pollute the coast and the ocean, and are one of the top ten items of rubbish found during coastal clean-ups.

The average straw is used for around twenty minutes before it is thrown away. Straws aren't reused or recycled. **20**

500 MILLION
The estimated number of plastic straws that are used every day in the USA. If you put this number of straws end to end, they could circle the planet more than two-and-a-half times!

100,000
The number of marine animals that are killed every year because of plastic rubbish. Seabirds, whales, dolphins and turtles are just some of the animals that eat plastic straws because they think they are food.

50–80% The amount of oxygen we get from the ocean. If the ocean suffers, so do we.

WHAT CAN YOU DO?
Say no to plastic straws and ask for a paper or bamboo one instead. These alternatives are made of natural materials and are easily recycled.

2 Read the text again. Are the sentences true (T) or false (F)? Correct the false sentences.
1. The Egyptians found insects inside their straws.
2. Early straws were made of glass.
3. People used to think straws were cleaner than cups and glasses.
4. Straws are one of the most common types of marine rubbish.
5. Nearly half of our oxygen comes from the sea.
6. There isn't a natural alternative to plastic straws.

3 🔊 7.8 Listen to Emily and Oscar talking. What's the name of the café they are in?

4 🔊 7.8 Listen again. Answer the questions.
1. What is unusual about the food the café serves?
2. What upset the two sisters about the food industry?
3. Are the prices on the menu?
4. What are the straws made of?
5. What will Oscar eat his ice cream with?

SPEAKING Agreeing and disagreeing

I can agree and disagree politely with another person.

1 🔊 **7.9** Listen and read. What type of party would Polly like this year?

> **Joel:** Have you decided what you're going to do for your birthday yet?
> **Polly:** Well, I'd like a party at home. It's more chilled.
> **Joel:** I totally agree. We can all bring food and drink.
> **Polly:** That's true, but I've had an idea. How about a plastic-free party? There was a lot of rubbish at the end of my party last year.
> **Joel:** You're right about that! But we can recycle the plastic plates and cups. It's easier than doing the washing up.
> **Polly:** Mm, I'm not sure I agree with you, Joel. We should all use less plastic.
> **Joel:** Well, yes, but it's difficult. I mean, everything is wrapped in plastic these days.
> **Polly:** I know, so we won't have crisps or snacks. But we can make pizzas. It'll be fun. Oh, and no balloons, please.
> **Joel:** But a party isn't a party without balloons.
> **Polly:** Sorry, but I don't agree. We can make paper lanterns instead. They can be reused at another party.
> **Joel:** That's a good point. I'm also going to recycle something really cool for your present.

2 🔊 **7.10** Listen and repeat the **Useful language**.

> **Useful language**
> **Agreeing**
> Yes, I agree (with you).
> That's true, but ...
> (Perhaps) you're right.
> I (totally) agree.
> That's a good point.
> I think that's a great idea.
> Absolutely!
> You're (definitely) right about that!
>
> **Disagreeing**
> Sorry, I don't agree.
> I don't think that's true.
> I'm not sure I agree (with you/that) ...

3 🔊 **7.11** Copy and complete the dialogue with phrases from the **Useful language** box. Listen and check.

> **Olivia:** Matt, I've got an idea. What about having a 'walk or cycle to school' week.
> **Matt:** I ¹... agree, we all need more exercise, but what about people who live a long way from school? Not everybody has a bike.
> **Olivia:** ²... point. Perhaps they don't have to take part. There are only a few people who live more than 1 km away.
> **Matt:** I don't think ³... . I know a few people who live out of town.
> **Olivia:** Perhaps you're right. Well, why don't we find out and talk to some teachers.
> **Matt:** I think ⁴... .
> **Olivia:** OK, I'll ask Mr Hughes. Will you ask around your class?
> **Matt:** ⁵...! Let's talk later.

4 Work in pairs. Prepare a new dialogue. Follow the **Speaking plan**.

> **Speaking plan**
>
> **Prepare**
> › Choose an idea and make notes.
>   - a day (picking up litter in the park)
>   - a party (to swap old clothes)
>   - an art workshop (to make things from rubbish)
> › Decide who is agreeing and disagreeing.
> › Use phrases from the **Useful language** box.
>
> **Speak**
> › Practise your dialogue.
> › Act out your dialogue.
>
> **Reflect**
> › Ask the class if they agree or disagree with your idea.
> › How can you improve next time?

👁 Now play *Keep moving!*

» FAST FINISHER

Write three questions for a survey of how people use and recycle things.

LS Language summary: Unit 7 **SB** p. 133

REAL CULTURE!

Animal protection

I can evaluate and compare factual information from different websites.

From very small to very big – many wild animals are fighting for survival. Climate change, the destruction of natural habitats for farming and homes, and intensive hunting are often the causes of the problem. However, conservation groups around the world are working hard to help these animals survive.

North American bison

Around 30 million North American bison once lived on the American plains. This large flat area is between the Rocky Mountains in the west and sides of the Missouri Valley in the east. Although bison are able to run quite fast, they were once hunted for food and killed in huge numbers. By the beginning of the twentieth century, there were only a few hundred left. However, in recent years, animal groups have worked hard to protect them. Thanks to their efforts, the population has grown. Although they don't have as much freedom as they used to have, they are surviving in national parks and in wildlife areas. They are a 'keystone species'. This means they create and maintain an environment that many other creatures live in. In 2016, the bison also became a historical symbol of the United States, and now they are seen by many as symbols of strength, courage and inspiration. So, this species is playing an important role in the culture and lifestyle of the country, as well as protecting the environment.

Scottish wildcat

In Scotland, the wildcat is known as the 'Tiger of the Highlands'. This mysterious and secretive cat is one of the rarest animals in the world. They used to live in forests all around Britain. However, with the disappearance of the forests due to human population growth, they moved further north and are now only found in the wild landscape of Scotland. They have been there for nearly 10,000 years, but they are now in danger. Some scientists think there are probably fewer than 100 alive today. As well as losing their natural habitat, wildcats have mixed with domestic cats, so pure wildcats could disappear in the next five years. However, animal protection groups are working hard with local communities to track and protect these animals. Recently, the discovery of two pure wildcat kittens excited these groups. The kittens could be vital to the conservation of the species, because one cat can produce up to 100 more. This may be the start of the cat's recovery.

1 Read the introduction on page 76. Why do some animals need protection?

2 🔊 7.12 Read and listen to the text, then look at the pictures on the websites. Answer the questions.
   1 Where do these animals live?
   2 What do they have in common?

3 🔊 7.12 Read and listen to the text again. Copy the fact file in your notebooks and complete it.

FACT FILE	BISON	WILDCAT
Where did they use to live?	¹ On the American plains.	² ...
Where do they live now?	³ ...	⁴ ...
Reason(s) for disappearance	⁵ ...	⁶ ...
How have animal protection groups helped?	⁷ ...	⁸ ...
What do they represent?	⁹ ...	¹⁰ The wild landscape and the rich history of Scotland.

4 **Word Power** Find the nouns related to the verbs in the articles. Copy the verbs and nouns in your notebooks and write a sentence with each one.

conserve   destroy   disappear
discover   protect   survive

5 Work in pairs and answer the questions.
   1 How does making the bison a symbol of the USA help protect the animal?
   2 What is a keystone species?
   3 Do you think the wildcat kittens will be the start of this cat's recovery? Why/Why not?
   4 Which other animal is the wildcat compared to?

6 🔊 7.13 Listen to friends, Amelia and Noah talking about sea turtles. Who wants to join the local animal protection group, Amelia or Noah?

7 🔊 7.13 Listen again. Answer the questions.
   1 Who gave the talk at Amelia and Noah's school?
   2 What two reasons explain the reduction in the number of sea turtles?
   3 What sort of film won the competition?
   4 How long have turtles been around?
   5 How long can turtles sleep in the water without breathing?
   6 Where is it necessary to protect turtles?
   7 What would Amelia and Noah like to do next Thursday?

8 **THINK CRITICALLY** Work in groups. Discuss the problem of plastic pollution.

   1 Is it a problem in your country?
   2 What is the government doing to prevent/reduce it?
   3 What are you doing to reduce plastic pollution?

9 **COMPARE CULTURES** In groups, find an animal that is in danger in your country. Make a fact file with as much information as you can. Tell the rest of the class about your animal.

👁 Now watch the culture video.

» **FAST FINISHER**
Make a list of things your school can do to help creatures in danger.

77

Taking responsibility

WRITING A for and against essay

I can write a for and against essay about the environment.

1 Read the essay title. Do you agree or disagree with the statement?

HUMANS ARE THE BIGGEST DANGER TO THE ENVIRONMENT. DISCUSS.

<u>We regularly hear news stories about</u> pollution, climate change and the extinction of wild animals. Although many people believe that humans are responsible for this destruction, there are also many people who are trying hard to protect the environment, too.

<u>On the one hand,</u> many problems are caused by humans. They destroy forests and build factories. As a result, animal habitats are destroyed, and animals aren't able to find food. <u>In addition,</u> rubbish pollutes the sea and poisons fish.

<u>On the other hand,</u> humans also work hard to protect nature. Wild animals are often helped by animal conservation groups. <u>What's more,</u> many young people care about environmental problems. They clean up their coasts and towns and also recycle their plastic, paper and glass. But everybody has to take care of the environment, not just a few people.

<u>To conclude, I agree that</u> humans have caused many environmental problems, and although many people are also now working hard to solve them, we need more people to do this. Our planet is changing, we all have to be more responsible for our actions.

2 Read the essay. Does the writer agree or disagree with the statement? What tells you that?

3 Look at the underlined words. Which phrase …
1 introduces the argument for something?
2 gives the writer's final opinion?
3 adds more information?
4 presents the topic?
5 introduces the argument against something?

4 The writer gives <u>two</u> reasons *for* and <u>two</u> reasons *against* the argument that humans are the biggest danger. Write them in your notebook.

5 Look at the **Useful language** box. Which phrases aren't in the essay?

> **Useful language**
> **Introducing the argument**
> We regularly hear news stories about …
> News stories regularly tell us that …
> Although many believe …, there are also …
> **Introducing a point on one side**
> On the one hand, …
> **Introducing a point on the other side**
> On the other hand, …
> **Your conclusion**
> In conclusion,
> To conclude, I agree/disagree that …

6 Read the **Look!** box. Find examples of some of these expressions in the essay.

> **Look!** Giving more information
> also   as well as …   in addition (to that) …
> too   what's more, …

7 Choose one of the topics. Write a for and against essay.
1 All schoolchildren should spend an hour a week picking up litter in their town. Discuss.
2 Too much money is spent on the protection of wild animals. Discuss.

> **Writing plan**
>
> **Prepare**
> › Make notes with your ideas.
>
> **Write**
> › Put your ideas in the correct order.
> › Use the ideas in the **Useful language** and Look! boxes.
>
> **Reflect**
> › Check your grammar for passive forms.
> › Use vocabulary from this unit.
> › Contrast ideas and add information where possible.
> › Include your opinion, but keep it clear and simple.

The learning zone

Vocabulary: Education words; Phrasal verbs **Grammar:** Past perfect simple; Modals of possibility and certainty **Speaking:** Asking for news and reacting **Writing:** A blog post

VOCABULARY Education words

I can talk about education and school life.

1 Look at the picture. How do you usually prepare for an exam?

'That's a great revision plan, Luke, but where are you going to start?'

2 Read the survey. In pairs, check the meaning of the blue words.

SCHOOL CENTRAL

The best days of your life? For this month's edition of School Central, we carried out a survey about your experiences of school. Here are some of your answers to our questions.

1. What do you do when you get your school **report**?
2. Is it easier to pay **attention** in the morning or the afternoon?
3. Do you make a **revision** plan when you have exams? Which **topics** do you study first?
4. Do you have optional subjects in your school **curriculum**?
5. How many subjects are on your **timetable**?
6. How could you improve your **memory**?
7. Who do you talk to if you get a bad **result** in a test or even **fail** it?
8. Do you like the challenge of giving a **presentation**?
9. What subjects have you made **progress** in? Which ones did you **pass**?
10. What was your biggest **achievement** last year?

3 🔊 **8.1** Match responses a–j with sentences 1–10 in the survey. Listen and check.

a Probably about nine, including P.E.
b Yes. This term I'm taking photography lessons.
c I read it quickly and then give it to my parents.
d I talk to my parents or my teacher.
e I won a prize for a painting I did in Art.
f I got good marks in English and History.
g I could test myself more often. That might help.
h Yes, I do. I revise the easy subjects first.
i In the morning, after a good breakfast!
j Definitely, because speaking in front of people gives you confidence.

4 🔊 **8.2** Listen to Emily and Matt. What were they given today?

5 🔊 **8.2** Listen again. Answer the questions.
1 Which subject did Matt do really well in?
2 Which subject didn't Emily do very well in? Why?
3 How does Matt remember facts for exams?
4 What subjects aren't easy for Matt to revise?
5 What does Emily want to learn from Matt?

6 Read the **Look!** box. Find the collocations in the text and complete 1–5.

> **Look!** **Collocations**
>
> Some verbs and nouns frequently go together.
>
> **get a report**   **get (good/bad) marks**
> give ¹ …   pass/fail ⁴ …
> improve (your) ² …   pay ⁵ …
> make ³ …

7 Work in pairs. Cover the answers in Exercise 3. Ask and answer the questions so they are true for you.

 Now watch the vlog.

▶▶ FAST FINISHER

Make a list of subjects and optional subjects you would like on your 'ideal' timetable.

LS Language summary: Unit 8 **SB** p. 134

A warm welcome

READING

I can use titles and headings to make predictions about content.

1 Look at the pictures. Have you ever been to a place like this?

2 Read the text and match the headings in the box with the paragraphs A, B, C.

| Useful skills | A different way to start the day | A multi-national environment |

It's freezing outside, but I got a warm welcome in Svalbard!

Hi! I'm Clara. I'm from the UK, but for the next six months, I'm at school in Svalbard, Norway. The mountains are covered in snow and it's -13°C! Yesterday was my first day at Longyearbyen school – the most northern school in the world.

A ...
Before I got to the school, I had already noticed lots of people on skimobiles, but I was surprised to see a line of parked snowmobiles in the car park. Had some of the students driven to school? Yes, they had! Getting to school can be a real challenge when there's snow and ice everywhere. I was glad I had worn my favourite thermal jacket – it was freezing!

When I looked out of the window during the first class, I was amazed. It's hard to pay attention when you're so close to a real reindeer. Reindeer are not the only wild animals in the area. I was told polar bears had come into the town a few months ago!

B ...
I got my new timetable and went to my first class. I hadn't expected the school to be so multicultural. There are thirteen different nationalities here, including Russian, Thai and Chilean. New families come for work in the area, but they don't stay for a long time, so a new school year often means new faces in the classroom for the teacher. Despite this, students make lots of progress here.

C ...
Longyearbyen has fewer pupils than my secondary school in England. It also combines primary and secondary education so pupils in different year groups hang out together. We follow the same curriculum as other schools in Norway, but there are also extra subjects, like survival skills for students over sixteen. I met someone who had done the course last year. He learned how to behave near polar bears and how to deal with avalanches. I want to do the course next month, and I hope I don't fail because bears and avalanches are real dangers here.

It's exciting to be in a place that's so different. I can't wait to see what will happen tomorrow!

3 🔊 8.3 Answer the questions. Listen and check.
1 What is unique about Longyearbyen school?
2 Why are there 'new faces' in the classroom each year?
3 How is Longyearbyen different from Clara's school in England?
4 Which optional subject does Clara talk about?
5 Why is that subject important?
6 How does Clara feel about going back to school tomorrow?

4 **Word Power** Find words in the text related to snow, winter and cold weather. Add more words to the list.

freezing, skimobile ...

5 🌐 **COMPARE CULTURES** In pairs, look at the three headings and think about your situation. How do students get to school, where do the students come from and what extra skills can you learn?

FUN FACT In Longyearbyen, the sun sets around the end of October and doesn't rise again until after the middle of February!

80

GRAMMAR Past perfect simple

I can use the past perfect simple.

👁 Now watch the grammar animation.

1 Read the grammar box and complete the rules.

Affirmative	Negative
Before I got to the school, I **had noticed** lots of people on skimobiles. He **had** already **done** a survival skills course last year.	I **hadn't expected** the school to be so multicultural.
Questions	**Short answers**
Had some of the students **driven** to school?	**Yes**, they **had**. **No**, they **hadn't**.

Rules

We use the past perfect simple to talk about actions that happen [1] *before / after* another action in the past.

We form the past perfect simple with [2] *have / had* and the past participle.

We often use the past perfect simple and the past simple in the same sentence. We use the [3] *past simple / past perfect simple* for the action that occurred at an earlier time.

2 Complete the sentences with the past perfect simple.

By ten o'clock this morning ...
    Tia *had arrived* (arrive) at school.
1 Saul ... (not eat) his snack.
2 we ... (have) our first class.
3 our teachers ... (not give) us any homework.
4 I ... (collect) my report from the teacher.
5 my friend ... (text) me about a party.
6 Jo ... (play) football in P.E.
7 I ... (not show) my report to my parents!

3 Write questions and short answers with the past perfect simple.

    the party / start / when / Sam / arrive?
    Had the party started when Sam arrived?
    Yes, it had.
1 she / already leave / for school / when / you text her? ✓
2 the students / study this / before? ✗
3 you / finish / your test / when / the bell ring? ✓
4 the teacher / give the students / too much homework? ✗
5 he / borrow a book / from you before? ✓
6 Sarah / hear the song / on the radio? ✓

4 🔊 8.4 Complete the texts with the past perfect simple of the verbs. Listen and check.

cut   finish   happen   make   not have
not hear   read   ~~revise~~   send

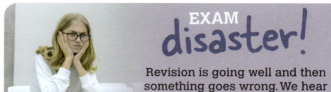

EXAM disaster!

Revision is going well and then something goes wrong. We hear some of your true stories.

The night before my French exam, I went to the park. I *'d revised* a lot for the exam, so I needed a break. Somebody [1] ... the grass. It smelled lovely! All of a sudden I couldn't stop sneezing. I [2] ... hay fever before. The next day my eyes were still red, but I answered all the questions between sneezes!

Last week, our teacher gave us an exam on one of the books we [3] ... in class. I knew I [4] ... a mistake when I saw the first question. I [5] ... the teacher properly and had revised the wrong book! I felt really stupid.

I woke up on the day of my last exam and saw that my friend [6] ... ten messages to me. She was at school and wanted to know what [7] ... to me. Then I saw the time – ten o'clock! Everybody [8] ... the exam when I arrived. My teacher wasn't very happy with me.

5 Work in pairs. Describe a time when something went wrong at school. Use the past perfect simple.

6 Complete the sentences with the correct past perfect simple or past simple form of the verbs.

    Jen ... (remember) that she ... (not buy) a birthday present for her mum.
    Jen remembered that she hadn't bought a birthday present for her mum.
1 The concert ... (not finish) when we ... (leave).
2 ... they ... (fly) before they ... (go) to London?
3 We ... (arrive) at the train station at 9.03 a.m., but the train ... (already / go).
4 Joe ... (fail) his Geography exam because he ... (not study) enough.
5 I ... (want) to call you, but Sam ... (not give) me your phone number.
6 ... you ... (finish) your homework before you ... (go) out?

» **FAST FINISHER**

How many ways can you complete the sentence using the past perfect simple?

I felt (adjective) yesterday because ...

LS Language summary: Unit 8 **SB** p. 134

It could be fun!

VOCABULARY and LISTENING Phrasal verbs

I can recognize a speaker's attitude and feelings.

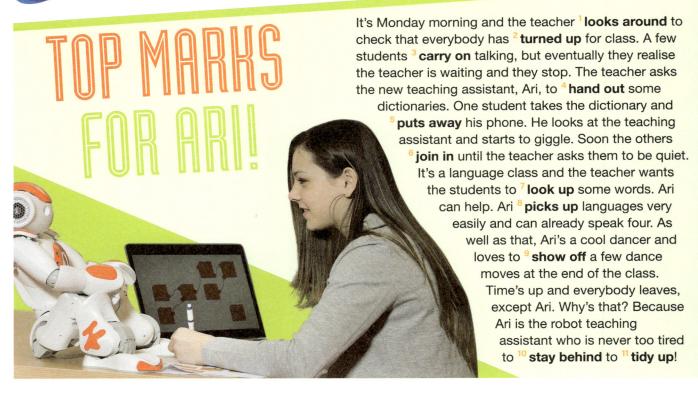

It's Monday morning and the teacher ¹**looks around** to check that everybody has ²**turned up** for class. A few students ³**carry on** talking, but eventually they realise the teacher is waiting and they stop. The teacher asks the new teaching assistant, Ari, to ⁴**hand out** some dictionaries. One student takes the dictionary and ⁵**puts away** his phone. He looks at the teaching assistant and starts to giggle. Soon the others ⁶**join in** until the teacher asks them to be quiet. It's a language class and the teacher wants the students to ⁷**look up** some words. Ari can help. Ari ⁸**picks up** languages very easily and can already speak four. As well as that, Ari's a cool dancer and loves to ⁹**show off** a few dance moves at the end of the class. Time's up and everybody leaves, except Ari. Why's that? Because Ari is the robot teaching assistant who is never too tired to ¹⁰**stay behind** to ¹¹**tidy up**!

1 Work in pairs. Make a list of what you can use robots for.

2 🔊 **8.5** Listen and read the text. Then match phrasal verbs 1–11 with definitions a–k.
  a to arrive
  b to begin to do something that other people are already doing
  c to place (something) in a cupboard or on a shelf
  d to learn quickly by listening or watching people doing something
  e to find information about something in a book or online
  f to do something to attract attention and interest
  g to see what is nearby
  h to remove rubbish and put things in the right place
  i to remain in a place after others leave
  j to give something to individuals in a group
  k to continue (doing something)

3 Complete the sentences with a phrasal verb.
  1 I'm quite tidy and usually ... my clothes.
  2 I often ... to do homework in the library.
  3 My brother ... by singing when we have guests.
  4 I don't ... languages very quickly. I find them difficult.
  5 If my friends are chatting, I always like to ... the conversation.
  6 It's annoying when friends ... late for the cinema and we miss the start of the film.

4 Work in pairs. Are the sentences in Exercise 3 true for you?

5 🔊 **8.6** Listen to three dialogues. Choose the correct answers.
  1 Jess and Ahmed *are in class / have just had a class* with a robot.
  2 The robot helps *Sam / Rachel*.
  3 Mia and Lucas are sure the *robot / teacher* will be funny.

6 🔊 **8.6** Listen again. In pairs, answer the questions.
  1 How does Ahmed feel about a robot in class?
  2 Why does Jess change her opinion about robots in class?
  3 Why doesn't Sam want to speak to the robot?
  4 How does Rachel feel about the robot's actions?
  5 Why isn't Mia excited about the idea of a robot in class?
  6 What isn't Lucas sure about?

7 💭 **THINK CRITICALLY** What are the advantages of having robots in a school? What jobs can they do in school? Which lessons would a robot be useful for and why?

>> **FAST FINISHER**
Write sentences about what happened at the beginning of your lesson. Use the phrasal verbs.

LS Language summary: Unit 8 **SB** p. 134

GRAMMAR
Modals of possibility and certainty

 I can use modal verbs to talk about possibility and certainty.

👁 Now watch the grammar animation.

1 Read the grammar box and complete the rules.

> Robots **can** be very useful in the classroom.
> It **could** be really good fun.
> The robot **might** help you.
> We **may** have a robot teaching assistant next week.
> It **must** be really strange for her.
> You **can't** be serious.
>
> **Rules**
>
> We use *can* when something is generally possible.
>
> We use *could/might/may* + verb for things that are possible in the ¹ *past / future*.
>
> We use *must, might, may* and *could* to speculate about the present and future.
>
> We use *must* when we are ² *certain / not certain* about something. We use *might, may* and *could* when are ³ *sure / not sure*.
>
> We use *can't* when something is ⁴ *possible / not possible*.

2 Read the email and choose the correct answers.

> Hi Ella,
>
> Thanks for your message! You're lucky you've only got one more exam. I've got three! You ¹ *must / might* be happy that you've nearly finished. It ² *might / can't* be easy to find time for revision when you're also in the school play.
>
> I'm looking forward to seeing you next month. Would you like to come to the school concert with me? It ³ *might / can't* be a bit boring, but at least you'll see my school and meet my friends. I ⁴ *may / must* have after-school activities on some days. You ⁵ *could / can't* join in if you like tennis and dancing.
>
> I'm going to a Zumba class now. Some exercise ⁶ *must / might* help me focus on my revision!
>
> Charlotte

3 PRONUNCIATION Sentence stress

🔊 **8.7** Listen to the following sentences. Are the modal verbs stressed or unstressed?

You must be happy with your result.
That can't be good for your eyes.

4 🔊 **8.7** Listen and repeat.

5 Complete the second sentence so that it means the same as the first.
1. I think Max has an exam today, but I'm not sure.
   Max … an exam today. (could)
2. It's possible I'll stay behind at school today.
   I … behind at school today. (may)
3. I'm sure this is the right address.
   This … the right address. (must)
4. I'm sure these instructions are wrong.
   These instructions … right. (can't)
5. Perhaps we'll get our exam results today.
   We … our exam results today. (might)

6 Read the news story. Complete the comments with the words in the box.

> can find   can't be   ~~could be~~
> may prefer   must feel

TWIN POWER!

A school in North America has broken a record for having 44 pairs of twins in the same school year. Is it fun or is it double trouble? We asked students what they think about it.

Comments

 I'm not sure about it. It could be confusing for everybody if the twins are identical.
♡ 6   ⇄ 2

 Some twins ¹… to be in separate classes, so that they can meet other people.
♡ 20   ⇄ 9

 Twins ²… it hard to make friends when they're together all day and only talk to each other.
♡ 3   ⇄ 1

 It ³… fun all the time. What happens when you have an argument with your twin?
♡ 18   ⇄ 4

 They're lucky! They ⁴… happy because they've always got a friend to talk to.
♡ 9   ⇄ 2

7 In pairs, discuss the story in Exercise 6. What might it be like to be a twin?

» **FAST FINISHER**
Write sentences about where your family members are at the moment. Use *could/may/might/can't* and *must*.

LS Language summary: Unit 8 **SB** p. 134

Did you hear about ...?
READING and LISTENING

I can identify whether events are in the past or future.

1 Work in pairs. Look at the activities in the box that some people do at school. Which do you take part in? Which do you enjoy the most? Why?

art exhibitions   clubs   concerts   plays   sports

2 Read the e-newsletter. Which events have already happened?

art exhibition   drama workshop   Maths teacher leaving   parents' evenings   sports awards

Head teacher's letter

Welcome to our May newsletter. Our pupils and teachers have been very busy, as you can see.

Many pupils are revising for GCSE and IB exams this term. There are quiet study areas in the library and common room for these pupils. Please respect them.

Wishing you all a happy and successful month,

K Brightman, Head Teacher

Follow us on social media!

Art exhibition

Our annual school art exhibition opens on 12 May. This year's theme is a quote by Matisse: *Creativity takes courage*. The Art Department has encouraged pupils to be adventurous with their ideas and their use of colour. The results are amazing!

Come along and bring parents and friends!

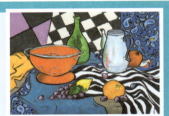

'Creativity takes courage'
Henri Matisse

Sports awards

Special congratulations to the winners from the sports awards evening last week. Well done on your achievements!

Click here to see more photos. >>

Drama workshop

The GCSE Drama group had a great day at the Attic Theatre for a workshop on Masks and Movement.

We looked at ancient Chinese masks online, but we hadn't worn them before. It was quite strange at first!

Celia Moore, Class 9C

The masks weren't comfortable. I think it must be hot to wear the masks for a whole show, but we enjoyed creating a scene.

Dan Young, Class 9D

Actors from the theatre taught us how to move to match the character of the masks. I hadn't realized how much fun masks could be!

Abigail Jones, Class 9B

Goodbye!

Sadly, Mr Russell is leaving at the end of term, so there'll be a special assembly for him in the last week. Anybody who wants to be involved should see Mr Andrews in the staffroom at break times.

Dates for your diary

Parents' evenings will be held from 15–19 May. Your parents can book appointments with your teachers online. The school has emailed your parents, but please remind them!

3 🔊 8.8 Listen to three dialogues. Which headings from Exercise 2 are the speakers talking about?

4 🔊 8.8 Listen again. Answer the questions.
  1 What was the prize for?
  2 Why might the teacher be leaving? What reasons do you hear?
  3 What is the girl's favourite subject?

5 What has happened or will happen at your school this term / this year? In pairs, compare your answers.

Our History teacher left at the end of last term.
There will be a parents' evening next month.

SPEAKING
Asking for news and reacting

I can ask for and react to news.

1 In pairs, look at the pictures. What do you think the students' news is about?

2 🔊 8.9 Listen and read the dialogue. Why hasn't Lara heard the latest school news?

> **Stefan:** Hey, Lara! What have you been up to? I haven't seen you around.
> **Lara:** I was playing in a basketball tournament. We got back late. We won though!
> **Stefan:** That's brilliant! Well done!
> **Lara:** Thanks. Have I missed anything?
> **Molly:** Have you heard about the reporter who was in school yesterday?
> **Lara:** A reporter? No way! What happened?
> **Molly:** She came to interview our new music teacher. Apparently, she was in a band a few years ago.
> **Lara:** Really? You're joking! Which one?
> **Stefan:** It says on the school website. I can't remember it. She used to be quite famous.
> **Lara:** Wow! I didn't even know there was a new music teacher! Anyway, did you have a good weekend?

3 Read the dialogue. Who …
1 asks for news?
2 congratulates the other speaker?
3 gives news?
4 is surprised by news?

4 🔊 8.10 Listen and repeat the **Useful language**.

Useful language
Asking for news
What have you been up to?
Have I missed anything?
Did you have a good weekend?

Giving news
Apparently, …
It says … here / on the website.
Have you heard about …?

Reacting
That's (+ adjective).   Really?
No way!   You're joking!
What happened?   I didn't (even) know …

5 🔊 8.11 Read the dialogues between Tom (T) and Mason (M). Choose the best responses. Listen and check.

1 **M:** Hi, Tom. Did you have a good weekend?
  T: It was OK, but when I came home from football training nobody was in and I hadn't taken a key! I had to sit outside for an hour until my dad got home!
  M: a What happened?
       b Oh no! You're joking!
       c That's brilliant!

2 **M:** Have you heard about the school website? They're looking for pupils who can help to improve it.
  T: a Really? I didn't know that.
       b Oh dear. That's awful!
       c Have I missed anything?

3 **M:** Apparently, the head teacher wants people to write articles for the news page. I'm going to go to a meeting about it. What do you think?
  T: a What happened?
       b Did you know about it?
       c Really? That's interesting.

6 Work in pairs. Prepare and practise a dialogue. Choose a type of news from the list. Follow the steps in the **Speaking plan**.

personal news	school news
visit cousins	sports team wants new players
go for a run	a history trip
art homework	a new teacher
win a competition	a new club

Speaking plan

Prepare
› Choose a piece of personal news and a piece of school news for your dialogue.
› Make notes: is the subject of your news in the past or future?

Speak
› Practise your dialogue.
› Use phrases from the **Useful language** box.
› Act out your dialogue without notes.
› Choose another situation and swap roles.

Reflect
› Did you use energetic intonation to respond to news?
› Did you use tenses correctly?
› How can you improve next time?

● Now play *Keep moving!*

» FAST FINISHER
Write a short news update for a school website. It can be real or imagined. Start with *Apparently …* or *Have you heard …?*

LS Language summary: Unit 8 SB p. 134

REAL CULTURE!

Learning together

I can make connections between paragraphs and pictures.

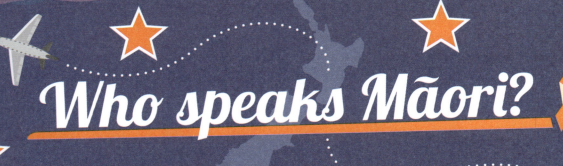

Who speaks Māori?

A Like many countries, New Zealand has people who come from different cultural backgrounds. The two main groups are Māoris, and other New Zealanders, whose parents and grandparents mainly come from Europe. In order to understand why New Zealand has two cultures, you need to go back in time. In 1250, Māori people travelled there in boats from other Pacific islands. They called their new home Aotearoa, or 'Land of the Long White Cloud'.

B At that time, Europeans hadn't discovered these two large islands in the southern hemisphere. They didn't arrive until the seventeenth century. When they got there, they took over and changed the islands' name to New Zealand. In the centuries that followed, European 'Kiwis' paid little attention to Māori culture. But in 1989, a new law was passed which made learning about it part of the school curriculum, and bicultural education was introduced. This was a real achievement, but what have been the results so far?

C These days, schools recognize Māori culture and world view. Many primary school pupils have Māori language lessons and art lessons. They might cover the topic of the eight important shapes in Māori art. Or they may learn how Māori artists carve green stone into these shapes and discuss the meaning each shape has. For example, a curled leaf shape means 'the beginning of life'.

D During their time at secondary school, some students build their own marae. This is a special Māori meeting area with a big hall for events like celebrations, educational visits and sharing Māori culture. Students often comment on how this large, open space improves their learning. Here, students are free to move or sit on the floor with classmates and the atmosphere is more relaxed. In the Māori language, *teach* and *learn* are the same word: ako. Teachers are not expected to know everything, so learning is often a shared experience, and the relationships between students and between student and teacher are important.

E Māoris have always used songs and movements to tell stories and pass on traditions. Most New Zealand pupils learn traditional Haka (Māori dances). Dancing in large groups helps students to learn the key life skill of working together, which is also a Māori ideal. Nowadays, many schools create their own Haka with words and movements that have a special meaning to them.

1 In pairs, take turns to describe one of the pictures of New Zealand 1–4. What does it show?

2 🔊 8.12 Read and listen to the article. Match pictures 1–4 with four of the paragraphs A–E.

3 Match paragraphs A–E with topics 1–5. Give examples from the text.
   1 Two ways traditions are passed on.
   2 A place where students can practise and talk about their culture.
   3 The first people who came to New Zealand.
   4 An example of Māori culture which young students might learn.
   5 The reasons why New Zealand schools are bicultural.

4 Are the statements true (T) or false (F)? Correct the false statements.
   The first people to live in New Zealand were Europeans. F
   1 The Europeans changed the country's name to New Zealand.
   2 Kiwis have paid little attention to Māori culture since 1989.
   3 There are eight important shapes in Māori art.
   4 Students comment that knowing about Māori art and language improves their learning.
   5 Students visit a *marae* for special events.
   6 Teachers must know everything that they teach to their students.
   7 Māoris consider 'learning together' to be an important life skill.
   8 Students work together and come up with their own individual dances.

5 **Word Power** Look at the text and find words and expressions related to time and periods in life.
   go back in time

6 💡 **GET CREATIVE** Copy the mind map. Choose a few learning areas and add examples of topics or skills that are important to you.

Work in pairs. Discuss your mind map and which subjects don't just teach facts, but also culture.

7 🔍 **FIND OUT** New Zealanders call themselves *Kiwis*. What kind of animal is a kiwi? What are its habits and why is it special to this country?

👁 Now watch the culture video.

≫ **FAST FINISHER**
Write sentences about your favourite learning areas. Use the mind map in Exercise 6 for ideas.

Let me tell you about …

WRITING A blog post

I can use informal register in a blog post.

1 Read the blog post. Why were the pupils surprised?

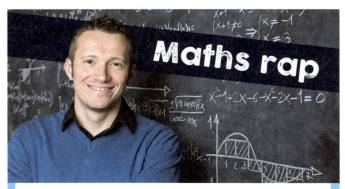

Has a teacher ever surprised you? This morning, our Maths teacher showed off a new skill. Let me tell you about the lesson. It started like any other. I was two minutes late and I turned up just as Mr Kent was handing out our homework papers. Next, he just took a deep breath and started rapping. Amazing!

The rap was about our Maths revision. He'd written it himself and it was brilliant!

While he was rapping, I looked round the class and everybody was laughing and clapping. I couldn't believe it! What a cool teacher!

It turns out he had looked at some Maths raps online and they gave him the idea. What's more, we all joined in, so now we know that lesson really well. Guess what? Next week we're going to make our own raps for a public competition. How exciting! But also, how scary!

Have you got any teacher stories to share? I'd love to hear all about them!

2 In pairs, find the phrases which show the writer's reactions and opinions. What do you notice about the punctuation?

3 Look at the **Useful language** box. How do you say these expressions in your language?

Useful language
Asking informal direct questions
Has a teacher ever surprised you?
Guess what?
Have you got any teacher stories to share?
Talking to your audience personally
Let me tell you about …
I'd love to hear all about …
Informal storytelling phrases
Well, this morning …
Next, …
It turns out (that) …

4 Read the **Look!** box. Why do we use this type of phrase in informal writing?

Look! Exclamatory phrases
Amazing!
How exciting!
What a cool (teacher)!
I couldn't believe it!
I'd love to (hear them / see it)!

5 In your notebooks, copy and complete the sentences with the phrases in the box. Match the sentences with a reaction (a–e).

a surprise trip to the sea
did an amazing Samba dance
passed my music exam
the school play is brilliant
there are 52,000 students at one school

1 Our teacher …
2 The sports club is planning …
3 I … with the top grade.
4 I've heard …
5 Did you know that … in Lucknow, India?

a How exciting!
b I'd love to see it!
c What a cool teacher!
d Amazing!
e I couldn't believe it!

6 In pairs, write an informal blog post about something surprising that happened to you. Follow the steps in the **Writing plan**.

Writing plan

Prepare
> With a partner, discuss ideas for your blog.
> Share ideas. Choose the idea you will write about.

Write
> Organize your ideas:
  - what happened first?
  - how did you react?
  - how did other people react?
  - what direct questions can you ask your reader?
> Use expressions from the **Useful language** box.

Reflect
> Read your blog post aloud. Does it use informal register?
> Does it use contractions, and does it sound like you are speaking?
> Check that you have used question marks (?) and exclamation marks (!) correctly.

W Writing summary: WB p. 91   E Exams: Unit 8 SB p. 125   LS Language summary: Unit 8 SB pp. 134

Your choice

Vocabulary: Shopping nouns; Adjectives and affixes | **Grammar:** Reported speech; Reported questions | **Speaking:** Persuading | **Writing:** A review

VOCABULARY Shopping nouns

I can describe different shopping experiences.

1 Work in pairs. Compare the pictures of two ways of shopping below. What are the differences?

2 🔊 9.1 Read the infographics. Copy and complete the sentences with words from the boxes. Listen and check.

| assistant | checkout | customers |
| payment | products | refund |

| chains | delivery | offers |
| purchase | receipts | service |

ADVANTAGES OF OFFLINE SHOPPING

1 … can share their experience with friends.

2 There's an … if you have any questions.

3 You can touch … . You can also try on clothes, like jeans and shoes, to help you decide.

4 You can see the product before you make a … .

5 You have the items that you've bought as soon as you have paid at the … .

6 It's easy to return the product and get a … if it's not what you want.

ADVANTAGES OF ONLINE SHOPPING

7 There are no queues, so … is usually quick.

8 You can find any shop online from big … to small stores.

9 It's easy to find great prices and special … .

10 You can stay at home and make a … at any time of day or night.

11 There's a record of your payment, so you don't need to keep … .

12 It's easy to send gifts as you can arrange … to any address.

3 🔊 9.2 Listen to two dialogues about shopping and answer the questions.
1 What did Ted and Alisha want to do?
2 Why didn't Ted succeed?
3 What was the problem with Alisha's online purchase?

4 💬 **THINK CRITICALLY** In pairs, think of a disadvantage for each type of shopping. Share your ideas with the class.

I like shopping with friends. I can't do that online.

5 Do a class survey. Find which way of shopping is the most popular and why.

👁 Now watch the vlog.

» **FAST FINISHER**
Write five sentences about why you usually return goods or why you don't return them.

LS Language summary: Unit 9 SB p. 135

89

The Teenage Market

READING I can scan to find specific information.

1 Look at these headings in a report. What do you think the report is about?

Sellers and stalls   Entertainment   Where did it all start?
Happy ending   What do teenage shoppers look for?

2 🔊 9.3 Read the text. Match the headings with A–E in the text. Listen and check your answers.

A …
Two teenage brothers from Stockport in England, Tom and Joe Barratt, came up with the idea for The Teenage Market in 2012. Most markets are in one place and are regular events. The Teenage Market is different. It's not one market, but individual events in different towns where creative teenagers can sell products which they've made themselves. Tom and Joe's vision for a new shopping experience has spread to over 30 towns. It's 9 a.m. on a Saturday, and today's market is already busy with young sellers who are setting up their stalls.

B …
At today's event, eleven teenagers are selling alongside stallholders who attend the regular weekly market. One girl, Becky, told me that over 70 young sellers had applied to take part in the first event. She said one reason for the popularity was that young people didn't have to pay for their stalls. At first, some regular traders said they didn't want Teenage Market traders to have free stalls. Now they don't mind because when there's a Teenage Market event, more people come to shop!

C …
I asked young sellers around the country for their opinions. Jay sells mobile phone cases with his own artwork on them. 'My friends say that they love to meet up and hang out at the markets. They like the atmosphere as well as the cool products and great performers!' Martha upcycles clothes for her recycled clothing stall. She takes old material and turns it into her own designs. In her opinion, 'Young people have been fed up with big chains for some time. My customers prefer sustainable shopping and personal service. They love my special offers, too.'

D …
The Teenage Market experience is definitely more fun than most markets because young entertainers are also taking part. According to one singer, the organizers said they were looking for performers. 'I messaged them and here I am!'

E …
So, are Tom and Joe happy with their idea? Of course! Joe said that the response to The Teenage Market had been amazing and it had given the young traders a real start in their creative careers.

3 Read the text again. Are the sentences true (T) or false (F)? Correct the false sentences.

The Teenage Market was started by teenagers for teenagers. T

1 The markets started in Stockport in England.
2 Teenage Markets are held every week.
3 Regular market holders have always welcomed Teenage Market traders.
4 Martha makes new clothes from old ones.
5 Most stallholders are also performers.

4 **Word Power** Find and complete the phrasal verbs from the text. Write sentences with them.

set …   come …   meet …
hang …   take …   turn …

5 💡 **GET CREATIVE** In pairs or small groups, come up with a product you could make and sell at the Teenage Market. Describe your product in detail: what it is, what it's made of, who would make it and why people would buy it.

GRAMMAR Reported speech

 I can report what people have said.

● Now watch the grammar animation.

1 Read the grammar box. Copy and complete the direct and reported speech from each person.

Direct speech	Reported speech
Present simple	**Past simple**
We **don't want** traders to have free stalls.	They said (that) they **didn't want** traders to have free stalls.
Present continuous	**Past continuous**
We **are looking** for performers tomorrow.	They said (that) they ¹… for performers the next day.
Present perfect	**Past perfect**
Martha: Young people ²… fed up with big chains.	Martha said (that) young people **had been** fed up with big chains.
Past simple	**Past perfect**
Becky: Over 70 young sellers **applied** to take part.	Becky told me (that) over 70 young sellers ³… to take part.

Rules

When we report what someone has said, we:
1 choose a reporting verb, such as *say* or *tell* and use it in the correct tense.
2 change the tense of the action back (e.g. *I am buying…* → *I was buying…*)
3 change the pronoun (e.g. *we* → *they*)
4 use a conjunction such as *if* or *that*, if necessary.
5 change the time expression (e.g. *tomorrow* → *the next day*)

2 Put the words in order to make sentences.
1 brother / My / me / that / told / hungry / was / he
2 that / My / said / want / friend / she / T-shirt / didn't / another
3 told / The stallholder / me / it / a / was / special offer
4 party / their / They / said / food / that / for / were / buying / they
5 not / Tilly / told / their / was / the class / well / teacher
6 leave / told / Dad / us / it / that / time / was / to
7 said / had / She / sold / hats / she / all / the

3 Rewrite the reported speech as direct speech. Change pronouns and possessive adjectives.

Jack said that he had made 50 picture frames to sell.
'I have made 50 picture frames to sell.'

1 April said that she was looking for a present for her dad.
2 Anna and Luke said they didn't like the live music.
3 Ben said he hadn't finished his shopping.
4 Sarah said she had been surprised that the service was so good.
5 Matt said that he enjoyed looking for special offers.

4 Report each statement using *said that*. Change the underlined words.

1 <u>I want</u> to get <u>my</u> lunch from the market. **Daisy**
2 <u>I tried</u> on some hand-painted trainers, but they were too small. **Dan**
3 <u>I haven't bought</u> a present for <u>my</u> mum. **Lily**
4 <u>I watched my</u> sister perform some new songs. **Max**
5 <u>Our cousins are</u> selling their artwork on a stall. **Poppy and Joe**
6 <u>We</u> don't often spend time on <u>this</u> beach with <u>our</u> friends. **Holly and Jacob**

5 In pairs, complete the sentences. Report what your partner said to the class.

Recently, I bought a/some …
It is/they are …
Andrea said that he had bought a hat.
He told me that it was for his brother.

» FAST FINISHER

Write three different endings for this sentence.
Yesterday, (name) told me that …

 Language summary: Unit 9 SB p. 135

Do the right thing

VOCABULARY and LISTENING Adjectives and affixes

I can take notes about the order of events.

1 In pairs, look at the pictures and the website. What is the website for?

2 🔊 9.4 Choose the correct answers for 1–6. Listen and check.

Freestuff.com

Have you got unwanted presents or stuff you don't need? Don't throw them away! Give them away or swap them.

Post a picture to find a new owner in your local area.

1 Who wants these socks? They're very *colourful / powerful*! They're too small for me. ♥ 16 likes

2 This pencil case is great and it's in *useful / reasonable* condition, too. I don't need it now. ♥ 9 likes

3 This used to be my favourite toy. It could be a *suitable / fashionable* present for a three-year-old child. ♥ 13 likes

4 My brother paints *wonderful / successful* pictures. He'll swap this for artist's paintbrushes. ♥ 22 likes

5 My gran wants to find a new owner for her vase. It's beautiful, but it isn't *comfortable / valuable*. ♥ 28 likes

6 Does anybody want my sister's bike? The paint is scratched, but it's very *reliable / helpful*. ♥ 35 likes

3 Which adjectives from Exercise 2 would you use to describe objects a–d from the Freestuff website?

4 🔊 9.5 Listen to the people talking. Which object is each person is describing?

5 🔊 9.6 Look at events A–D. Listen to a radio report. Number the events in the order they happened.
  A Robert phoned Customer Services.
  B The company found out what the problem was.
  C Many more products were delivered to Robert.
  D Robert received an unexpected package.

6 🔊 9.6 Listen again. Answer the questions.
  1 Why was Robert surprised to receive the first package?
  2 Was the Customer Services department helpful at first?
  3 What products were in Robert's deliveries?
  4 Why had the problem started?

7 Work in pairs. Have you ever received something you didn't want? Talk about what it was and what you did with it.

LS Language summary: Unit 9 SB p. 135

GRAMMAR Reported questions

 I can report questions people have asked.

● Now watch the grammar animation.

1 Read the grammar box. Copy and complete the rules.

Yes/No questions	
Direct questions	**Reported questions**
Reporter: **Are** you **going to keep** the products?	A reporter asked Robert **if/whether** he **was going to keep** the products.

Wh- questions	
Direct questions	**Reported questions**
Edward: What **have you received**?	He asked Robert **what** he **had received**.

Rules
We report *Yes/No* questions by using a past tense reporting verb (e.g. *asked*) + (person) + *if* or ¹... .

We report *Wh-* questions by using a past tense reporting verb (e.g. *asked*) + ²... (*who/what/when/where/how*).

2 Change the reported speech sentences to direct speech. Use the tense in brackets and change the pronouns.
1. The Customer Services department asked Robert what the problem was. (present simple)
2. The reporter asked if Robert was going to keep the products. (present continuous)
3. The company asked what products he had received. (present perfect)
4. The company said Robert could keep everything. (present simple)
5. The writer asked an expert if Robert had done the right thing. (past simple)

3 Read and complete the reported questions. Change any pronouns and possessive adjectives.

'Did you have a good day?'
My mum asked me *if I had had a good day*.

1. 'Where did you buy your T-shirt?'
   Sam asked me ... .
2. 'What did you give your mum for her birthday?'
   Dina asked me ... .
3. 'Are the shoes comfortable?'
   The shop assistant asked Sal ... .
4. 'Ben, what time is Jeff's party?'
   I asked ... .
5. 'Do you like my new bag?'
   Julia asked me ... .
6. 'Have you kept your receipt?'
   The shop assistant asked me ... .

4 🔊 9.7 Listen to Maya asking Carl about an article she has read. Which question don't you hear?

1. When did the boys start their company?
2. Is it a successful company?
3. Why do they design socks?
4. How many pairs of socks did Sebastian have when he was five?
5. What are they like?
6. How does the company help charities?

5 🔊 9.7 Listen again and answer the questions.

6 Report each question. Use *Maya asked if* or *Maya asked what/why/when …* .

Maya: When did the boys start their company?
Maya asked when the boys started their company.

7 In pairs, ask your partner one of these questions. Report the question to the class.
1. Do you like bright socks?
2. What did you do at the weekend?
3. What did you do yesterday evening?
4. Have you ever designed an item of clothing?

What did you do at the weekend?

Silvia asked me what I did at the weekend.

» **FAST FINISHER**
Write the questions that you asked your partner.
I asked (name) … .

 **Language summary: Unit 9** SB p. 135

KEEP TALKING!

You won't regret it!

READING and LISTENING

I can understand signs and notices.

1 Look at the signs and notices. Which do you see when shopping online, in a shop or both?

a
Self-service checkout this way

b
Next day delivery between 7 a.m. and 10 p.m. Available Monday to Sunday. Place your order by midnight Sunday to Friday or 8 p.m. on Saturday and we'll deliver the next day.

c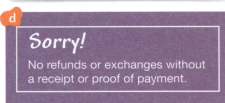
Please return your baskets here.

d
Sorry!
No refunds or exchanges without a receipt or proof of payment.

e
Any returned items must be unworn and unwashed with all original labels intact.

f
10% OFF FOR STUDENTS!
Sign up here for exclusive offers and discounts. Complete the form below with your name and address and we'll send you a unique shopping code.
SUBMIT

g
Special offer on all school bags.
Buy one, get the second half price.

h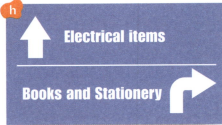
↑ Electrical items
Books and Stationery →

i
Home Deals Login
There is 1 item in your bag.

j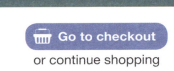
Clothes ▼ Footwear ▼ Account
🛒 Go to checkout
or continue shopping

2 Read the signs and notices again. Which …
1 offers lower prices if you are studying?
2 tells you not to take or send back dirty or used goods?
3 lets you see how many product(s) you have chosen?
4 explains when you will receive your goods?
5 offers you the option to pay or buy more?
6 gives you directions to different departments in a store?

3 🔊 9.8 Listen to Max and Cara. Where are they?
a a toy shop
b a department store

4 🔊 9.8 Listen again. Choose the correct answers.
1 Max has seen an offer for *cheap / free* cinema tickets.
2 The questionnaire is about people's *shopping / travel* experiences.
3 Cara needs *money / ideas* for her brother's birthday present.
4 She is going to the *toy / entertainment* department.
5 Cara *hopes / doesn't think* that Max will get the cinema tickets.

5 In pairs, discuss your favourite shop or type of store. Talk about what it is and why you like it.

FUN FACT
At a popular chain store a customer recently returned a shirt that was seventeen years old and was given a refund. The shop manager reminded the assistant that the shop's return policy was 45 days!

SPEAKING Persuading

I can use simple language to persuade others.

1 What things do you find at a second-hand market?

2 🔊 9.9 Listen and read the dialogue. What does Nathan persuade Alice to do?

Nathan: There's a second-hand market next Saturday. It's a great idea, isn't it?
Alice: I haven't really thought about it.
Nathan: Why don't you help me with it? Go on. It'll be fun!
Alice: Sorry, I don't think I can. I told my mum I'd go into town with her.
Nathan: That's a pity. It would be really helpful if you were there … just for an hour. Please say you'll come, Alice.
Alice: Well, I might come for an hour.
Nathan: In that case, why don't you come about nine o'clock?
Alice: I'll think about it, Nathan.
Nathan: Honestly, I think you'll enjoy it.
Alice: All right then, I'll do it. You couldn't sell some of my dad's old CDs, could you?
Nathan: Sure! Why not? Thanks, Alice! You won't regret it!

3 🔊 9.9 Listen and read again. Answer the questions.
1 Why can't Alice go to the second-hand market?
2 What does Nathan ask Alice to do?
3 What does Alice ask Nathan to sell for her?

4 Read the **Look!** box. Complete the sentences with a question tag.

> **Look!** Question tags
>
> We often use question 'tags' when we expect or want the other person to agree with us.
> If the sentence is affirmative, the tag is negative and if the sentence is negative, the tag is affirmative.
> *It's* a great idea, *isn't it*? *She didn't* pass, *did she*?

1 It's very colourful, …?
2 You haven't got the receipt, …?
3 It isn't very fashionable, …?
4 They can deliver seven days a week, …?

5 PRONUNCIATION Intonation

🔊 9.10 Listen to the two questions. Does the speaker's voice go up or down at the end?
That isn't very useful, is it?
I can pay with a card here, can't I?

6 🔊 9.11 Listen and repeat the **Useful language**.

> **Useful language**
>
> **Being persuasive**
>
> Are you sure you …?
> It would be really helpful if …
> Go on, it'll be …
> Why don't you …?
> Maybe we could …
>
> Honestly, I think you'll enjoy it.
> Please say you'll …
> You won't regret it!
> You'll have a great time!

7 🔊 9.12 Copy and complete the dialogue with words from the **Useful language** box. Listen and check.

Hannah: I need to get some things for my art project. It would be good if you could help me choose.
Anik: Oh, I'm sorry, but I'm busy today.
Hannah: Are ¹… you can't come? It won't take long.
Anik: I can't. I've got to look after my brother.
Hannah: ²… you bring him, Anik?
Anik: He doesn't like shopping very much. It's boring for him, isn't it?
Hannah: Maybe we could take him to the park afterwards? ³…, I think you'll both enjoy it. Please ⁴… you'll come, Anik.
Anik: Oh, all right. See you later.
Hannah: Thanks, Anik. You'll ⁵… time!

8 Work in pairs. Prepare a new dialogue to persuade a friend. Follow the steps in the **Speaking plan**.

> **Speaking plan**
>
> **Prepare**
> › Think of a situation or activity and decide why you want your friend to join you. Make notes.
> › Choose phrases from the **Useful language** box.
>
> **Speak**
> › Practise your dialogues.
> › Act out your dialogue without notes.
>
> **Reflect**
> › Swap roles and choose a different event.
> › How can you improve next time?

Now play *Keep moving!*

FAST FINISHER

Write a list of things that people usually need others to help them with.

LS Language summary: Unit 9 **SB** p. 135

REAL CULTURE!

Shopping adventure

I can follow the order of information in a text.

History | Attractions | Events | Getting there | **Shopping**

Fact File
OXFORD STREET

Where:	London's West End (Central London)
Length:	1.9 km
No. of shops:	Approximately 300
No. of visitors:	Four million each year
Transport:	24-hour Underground service available, Four Underground stations, regular bus routes
Opening hours:	Most shops are open from 9 a.m. to 9 p.m. Monday – Saturday and 12 p.m. to 6 p.m. on Sundays

Late-night shopping on Thursdays until 10 p.m.

Take a look at what makes a shopping experience on Oxford Street so special. Oxford Street is one of Europe's busiest shopping streets. Over the years, it has become known for its department stores, fashionable chain stores and trendy boutiques. The street generates around £5 billion in sales each year and is visited by around 600,000 shoppers every day. Around 30% of those visitors are from overseas.

The arrival of the first department stores on Oxford Street brought a new shopping experience to London. One of the first was Selfridges. This was opened by American businessman Harry Gordon Selfridge, in 1909. Harry Selfridge had been disappointed with the service in shops in England, so he decided to improve it. He wanted shopping to be an adventure and his store quickly became a successful business. At first, shoppers were surprised. They weren't used to being able to touch products and go to restaurants in shops, but they soon loved his ideas.

Advertising and special offers were used to attract customers and for the first time it was possible to enjoy 'just looking' at the products on sale. Selfridges was the first shop to put perfume near a door to attract people in!

Over the years, Selfridges has become famous for its elaborate window displays, especially before Christmas. It has managed to find different ways to make shopping interesting. Today, the store has a roof garden with a café, but in the past it has had an ice rink and even a mini boating lake with coloured water – the perfect place to have a break from shopping.

With the growth of shopping malls outside town centres and more people buying online, some shopping streets have seen a fall in the number of customers who shop in store. Fortunately, Oxford Street has great Underground and bus connections. But it is also very, very busy and noisy at times. However, this doesn't seem to put off the crowds who come every day, and the enormous number of visitors to Oxford Street shows that people still want what it offers.

9

1. Look at the pictures of Oxford Street and read the *Fact File*. Why do you think people shop there?

2. 🔊 9.13 Read and listen to the text. In your notebooks, make a list of things you can see or do in Oxford Street. Compare your ideas.

3. Read the text again. Find the information to complete the infographic.

OXFORD STREET
shopping central

The number of stores in Oxford Street: **300**

The number of people who visit Oxford Street every day: [1] ... .

Public transport: [2] ... trains and [3] ... .

The year Selfridges opened: [4] ... .

Ideas customers loved about Selfridges: [5] ... and [6] ... .

Why the number of customers has fallen: [7] ... and [8] ... .

4. **Word Power** Find examples of compound nouns in the text. Work in pairs and compare your lists.
shopping experience

5. 🔍 **FIND OUT** Oxford Circus is on Oxford Street. What is it and why is it called a circus?

6. 🌐 **COMPARE CULTURES** How is the shopping experience in Oxford Street similar to one you know? How is it different?

FUN FACT There are diagonal zebra crossings at Oxford Circus so people can cross in any direction. The design is the same as crossings in Tokyo.

7. Read the text about pop-up shops. Are the sentences true (T) or false (F)?
   1. Only big-name brands can set up a pop-up shop.
   2. Pop-up shops are expensive to run.
   3. Pop-ups are more popular with the younger generation.
   4. People tell each other about pop-ups shops.
   5. Pop-up shops can only open for two months.
   6. There is a pop-up shop for dogs in the UK.

POP-UP SHOPS!
DID YOU KNOW...?

1. Pop-up shops can be opened by anyone, at any time. They are a great way to find out if your product would sell in a shop long-term.

2. They can be a good, low-cost way to advertise a business and to get people interested in a new idea.

3. They can open in busy places, like shopping centres, but they can be in old buses, caravans or recycled shipping containers, too!

4. Pop-up shops often open at concerts, festivals and sporting events.

5. Pop-ups don't have to be shops – pop-up cinemas and restaurants are very popular, too!

6. Research shows that pop-up shops are most popular with 18–25-year-olds.

7. You can find out about pop-up shops on social media and also via word-of mouth. They can open from one day to three months – so you have to be quick!

8. Pop-up shops are not just for humans. BarkLive is a pop-up shop for dogs and puppies that opened in New York! Up to five dogs at a time can go into the shop and their owners can see which toys they like to play with. Maybe that one should be called a 'pup-up' shop?! Ha ha!

WOOF!!!

👁 Now watch the culture video.

» **FAST FINISHER**
Make a list of all the types of shops or buildings you can find on a busy high street.

97

Everything you need!

WRITING A review

I can write a review about a shop.

1 Look at the picture and read Toby's review. What can you buy in this type of shop? Give examples.

★★★★☆ Toby, 15

My favourite shop is definitely *Party Animal*. It's in a shopping mall out of town. A friend told me about it. He said it had everything you need for a birthday party and he was right!

The best thing about the shop is its range of products. It sells amazing costumes and masks, especially at carnival time. I love the wigs and I bought a long, purple one to wear at my party. I also find the shop assistants really helpful and patient when you can't decide what you want.

The main disadvantage is that the shop isn't on a bus route. It has a website, but it isn't very useful. It doesn't have the same offers and discounts and the delivery service isn't reliable. In my opinion, it's better to see the products in the shop.

To sum up, I would say that this shop has great party ideas at reasonable prices. I really think it's the best in this area. I would recommend it if you're planning a party or celebration.

2 Read Toby's review again and answer the questions.
1 How did he find out about *Party Animal*?
2 What two things does Toby like?
3 What two things does Toby not like?
4 Does Toby recommend the shop?

3 In pairs, discuss the questions.
1 Do you use shop reviews? Why/Why not?
2 What information do you look for in them?
3 Are online reviews always reliable?

4 Look at the **Useful language** box. What phrases does Toby use in the review?

Useful language
Writing a review
My favourite shop is …
The best thing about it is …
I (also) find … really helpful/useful.
The worst thing is …
The main disadvantage is that …
To sum up, I would say …

5 Read the **Look!** box. Copy and complete the sentences with the correct words.

Look! Recommending
I would/wouldn't recommend it.
It's really worth a visit.
You'll love it!
You won't be disappointed!

1 The food at the new café is wonderful. You … disappointed.
2 I always go to my favourite market on Sundays. It's really … a visit.
3 That new sports shop doesn't have a great choice. I … recommend it!
4 There's a fantastic music shop near my house. I think you'll … it.
5 I enjoyed our trip to the new department store in town. I … recommend it.

6 Write a review of a shop or a website. Follow the steps in the **Writing plan**.

Writing plan

Prepare
› Choose a shop or website.
› What is it called?
› How did you find out about it?
› Decide how many stars you are going to give it.

Write
› Use adjectives to describe the goods, the service, etc.
› Give reasons you like and don't like it.
› Use the expressions from the **Useful language** box.

Reflect
› Check your grammar: have you used the correct tenses?
› Have you included your opinion?
› Do you recommend the shop or website at the end of your review?

W Writing summary: **WB** p. 98
R Review: Units 7–9 **SB** pp. 104–105
P Project: Units 7–9 **SB** pp. 110–111
L Literature: Units 7–9 **SB** pp. 116–117
E Exams: Unit 9 **SB** p. 126
LS Language summary: Unit 9 **SB** p. 135

CONTENTS

REVIEWS
Units 1–3	Consolidation	p100
Units 4–6	Consolidation	p102
Units 7–9	Consolidation	p104

PROJECTS
Units 1–3	A blog post about the best tourist attractions in your region	p106
Units 4–6	A *How to ...* video	p108
Units 7–9	A design for a product made from recycled materials	p110

LITERATURE
Units 1–3	*The Canterville Ghost*	p112
Units 4–6	*Dr Jekyll and Mr Hyde*	p114
Units 7–9	*Frankenstein*	p116

EXAM PRACTICE
Unit 1	Reading: Multiple matching	p118
Unit 2	Listening: Multiple choice	p119
Unit 3	Speaking: Conversation	p120
Unit 4	Listening: Interview	p121
Unit 5	Listening: Sentence completion	p122
Unit 6	Writing: A story	p123
Unit 7	Reading: Multiple-choice cloze	p124
Unit 8	Speaking: Picture description	p125
Unit 9	Reading: Short texts	p126

UNITS 1–9 LANGUAGE SUMMARY	p127
IRREGULAR VERBS LIST	p136

REVIEW
UNITS 1-3

▶ READING

1 Choose the correct answers to complete the article.

ROLL UP, ROLL UP!

Giffords Circus [1] *has entertained / was entertaining* more than a million people since it [2] *began / was beginning* almost twenty years ago! Come along and watch our fantastic [3] *performances / performers* – we have jugglers, acrobats and the [4] *amazing / amazed* clown, Tweedy. Look out for the beautiful horses, too!

Why not eat in *Circus Sauce* – the UK's only travelling restaurant? The chef uses [5] *carnival / fresh* local ingredients and prepares meals for the [6] *parade / audience* to enjoy before or after a show. You can try some delicious [7] *homemade / ingredients* food from the pizza wagon or a freshly [8] *baked / stir-fried* cake during the interval.

[9] *Plan / Book* your tickets online now and avoid the [10] *seats / queues* when you [11] *arrive / depart* at the showground. We look forward to welcoming you and your friends and family for an evening full of fun!

2 Complete the comments with the words in the box.

costumes   disappointed   embarrassed
ever   haven't been   just   since   started
was waiting   went   were staying

🔊 I [1] … to a circus [2] … I was at primary school. But I've [3] … been to Giffords Circus. I wasn't [4] …! It was great fun. While I [5] … in the queue, a clown [6] … singing and dancing right in front me! I felt a bit [7] … and turned bright red! But he was funny! Try the pizzas from the pizza wagon – they're SO tasty!
Jody15

🟢 We [8] … to Giffords Circus last weekend while we [9] … with friends in Oxford. It's the best live show we've [10] … seen! The performers' colourful [11] … were incredible!
the Brown family

▶ LISTENING

3 🔊 **R1** Listen and match the people with the correct photo. There is one extra photo you do not need.

Carly   Josh   Ryan

a   b   c   d

4 🔊 **R1** Listen again and complete the sentences.
1 Carly went … for the first time.
2 Carly felt … about her family holiday.
3 Josh's grandma booked … for her whole family to go on holiday to New York.
4 Josh's grandma … him stories about her uncle.
5 Ryan bought a … taco from a street food stall.
6 Ryan's favourite snack was … and salty.

5 🔊 **R1** Are the sentences true (T) or false (F)? Correct the false sentences. Listen and check.
1 Carly packed her bag the night before her holiday.
2 Carly took the wrong wheelie bag at the airport.
3 Josh took part in a parade in New York.
4 Josh and his grandma were surprised at some information they discovered at the museum.
5 Ryan's taco had fried insects, creamy avocadoes and spicy chillies in it.
6 In Ryan's opinion, the fried insects were disgusting.

REVIEW Units 1–3

▶ SPEAKING

6 Work in pairs. Ask and answer the questions using the phrases below with the present perfect, *used to*, the past simple or the past continuous. Ask follow-up questions and find out more information.

HAVE YOU EVER
1 … (eat) an unusual snack?
2 … (watch) a frightening film?
3 … (make) your own pizza?

HAVE YOU
4 … (finish) your homework yet?
5 already … (have) your lunch?

WHAT
6 … you … (do) at 9 p.m. last night?
7 … you and your friends … (do) when your English lesson … (start)?

HOW LONG
8 … (know) your best friend?
9 … (live) in your house?

WHEN
10 … you … (be) at primary school, … you … (dress up) in costumes?

▶ WRITING

7 Write a paragraph to describe your best or worst holiday experience. Use the ideas below to help you.

Think about …
- the journey / transport
- the place
- the people
- an interesting event or entertainment
- the food / a special meal
- your feelings

TEST YOUR MEMORY!

- Say what you do before you go on holiday.
- Name five things you used to do when you were five.
- Make three questions with *How long …?* Give your answers with *for* and *since*.
- Describe three things that happened today. Use *-ed/-ing* adjectives.
- Describe a place you've never been to but want to go to.
- Say five ways you can cook chicken.
- Name five things you see at a carnival.
- Say three things you've already done today. Give details.
- Make three questions with *yet*.
- Describe what was happening when you arrived home from school yesterday.
- Name five things you see in a train station.
- Describe a snack you never eat. Say why you don't like it.

101

REVIEW
UNITS 4–6

▶ **READING**

1 Choose the correct answers to complete the text.

Home | **Jobs** | News | Sport | Trending

FUTURE EMPLOYMENT?

New technologies [1] *create / will create* up to 21 million new jobs by 2050. Here are the predictions about the jobs we [2] *will be doing / are doing* in the future.

IT and the car industry

There [3] *will be / won't be* any vehicles with drivers because driverless cars and drones will be using our roads and air space. People will develop technology for these vehicles, so they move [4] *carefully / carelessly* through our cities and don't have accidents. If you [5] *are / are going to be* interested in cars and technology, this might be a great job for you!

Environment

Do you like nature and wildlife? [6] *If / Unless* we plant more trees to create forests, carbon dioxide will increase in the atmosphere. We need more people to work in this sector! This is a great job for [7] *something / somebody* who loves nature, plants and animals. You [8] *should to / should* think about training for this job now – don't wait for the future!

Healthcare

If you were feeling ill, who [9] *do you ask / are you asking* for advice: a doctor? Well, in 2050, you probably [10] *wouldn't go / won't go* to see a doctor. When you want medical help or advice [11] *nowhere / anywhere* in the country (at home or on holiday), [12] *you'll talk / be talking* to a special computer with medical software. If you need medicine, the computer will send it to you immediately.

▶ **LISTENING**

2 🔊 R2 Listen. Which sport are Lisa and Kyle talking about?

a dodgeball

b cycle ball

c footvolley

3 🔊 R2 Listen again and complete the rules with the correct form of *can*, *be allowed to*, and *have to*.

1 You ... throw or catch the ball.
2 You ... use your hands or feet.
3 You ... only move or hit the ball with the bike.
4 You ... use your own bike.
5 You ... use a special bike.
6 You ... put your feet down during a match.
7 You ... score as many goals as you can in 40 minutes.

REVIEW Units 4–6

▶ SPEAKING

4 Work in pairs. Write one word for each prompt below. Make short notes for each one and take turns to ask and answer. Explain your reasons.

A: Who are you going to see later today?
B: Somebody I'm going to see later today is Ruben.
A: Who's Ruben?
B: He's my music teacher.

- Somebody I'm going to see later today.
- Somebody I argued with this week.
- Something I'll be doing when I'm 25.
- Somewhere I'll be going next weekend.
- Something that I find funny.
- Somebody I should get in touch with.
- Somewhere I hang out with friends.
- Something I'm not allowed to do but want to.
- Somewhere I want to go on my next holiday.
- Something I should do but don't.

▶ WRITING

5 Copy and complete the sentences for each topic.

Your dream job
When I finish school, I'm going to …
First, I'm going to …

Your ideal school rules
Students must … They don't have to …
Students are allowed to … They can … They can't …

Your favourite sport
In this sport, you need to …
You must … You mustn't …

Your family
If I argued with my …,
My parents say I have to …
I should … I shouldn't …

Your best friend
My best friend is … and …
I feel happy/confident/sociable/calm when …

TEST YOUR MEMORY!

- Say what you're going to do tonight and what you'll be doing at the weekend.
- Name five sports verbs.
- Describe yourself. Use adjectives of personality.
- Make sentences about obligation and advice. Use *must*, *need to*, *have to*, *should* and *ought to*.
- Say five things you don't have permission to do at school.
- Make three sentences starting *If/Unless …*
- Name five ways you can communicate with your classmates.
- Make sentences about your town. Use *who*, *which*, *where* or *that*.
- Name five nouns that end with -*ion*, -*tion* or -*sion*.
- Say five jobs. What sectors are they in?
- Give the adverb form of these adjectives: *bad*, *calm*, *good*, *lazy*, *terrible*.
- Give advice to your classmate on how to pass a test. Use *If I were you, …*

103

REVIEW
UNITS 7-9

▶ READING

1 Complete the blog post. Use the correct past perfect, present or past passive form of the verbs in brackets.

I didn't know that!

By Maisie Sheridan

I think almost everybody must have at least one pair of trainers in their wardrobe, so I decided to do some research. Here are the results – you may be surprised!

- Six out of ten pairs ¹ … (make) in China. More than 270,000 pairs ² … (sell) every day!

  That can't be true, or can it?

- In the 1800s, leather ³ … (use) to make sports shoes and they were very heavy. They didn't look very good, and they certainly weren't comfortable! Ouch!

- In 1907, the first basketball shoes ⁴ … (wear) by American basketball players.

  But in the USA, trainers ⁵ … (not call) trainers – they're sneakers!

- By 1950, teenagers ⁶ … (begin) to wear trainers to make a fashion statement.

- By 2017, Adidas ⁷ … (decide) to start making trainers from recycled plastic using plastic waste from beaches, which would otherwise pollute the oceans.

- In 2019, more than 11 million pairs of Adidas trainers ⁸ … (produce) using recycled plastic. By the end of the year, the company ⁹ … also … (collect) more than 40 tons of plastic waste from their offices and from purchases that ¹⁰ … (make) in their stores.

? What do you think of this? Can we save the planet and be fashionable? Or is it too little too late? What do you think? Post a comment now.

 Share  Like Comment

Comments

I think it's a good idea. Recyling plays a valuable role. We need to use recycled plastic in more products! **Marie45**

Now I've read this, I might buy some recycled ones. But I'll carry on wearing my old trainers until I need new ones. **@RedPanda7**

▶ LISTENING

2 🔊 R3 Listen and write down the topics from the box that Luke and Maya mention.

advice	curriculum	delivering newspapers	exams
homework	marks	memories	payments
reports	revision	sleep	timetable	waste

3 🔊 R3 Are the sentences true (T) or false (F)? Correct the false sentences. Listen and check.
1 Maya has just finished her exams.
2 She thinks it isn't a good idea to start revision too early.
3 Maya had enough time to revise because she had made a revision timetable.
4 She sometimes revised in the school library.
5 She doesn't think sleep is essential before an exam.
6 Maya doesn't know if she'll get good exam marks.

4 🔊 R3 Choose the correct words and write the correct form of the verbs in the box. Listen again and check.

| be | do | feel | have | not know |
| pass | revise | work |

First, Luke asked Maya ¹ *when / how* she ² … . Then he asked her ³ *whether / what* her top revision tips ⁴ … . She told him that she ⁵ … two top tips. Next, Luke asked her ⁶ *who / where* she had studied for her exams and Maya told him that she ⁷ … all her revision in the school library. After that, he asked her ⁸ *if / what* she ⁹ … hard, and she said that she ¹⁰ … a lot. Finally, he asked her ¹¹ *when / whether* she thought she ¹² … her exams. Maya told him that she thought she had, but she ¹³ … if she would get good marks!

104

REVIEW Units 7-9

▶ SPEAKING

5 Work in pairs. What do you think is happening in the picture? Use *could*, *may*, *might*, *can't* and *must*.

The children must be on a school trip.

6 What had they done by the end of the day? Make statements using the words in the box and the past perfect.

| eat / lunch | feed / animals | lose / phones |
| (not) pay attention to / signs | take / photos |
| throw away / rubbish |

▶ WRITING

7 Choose one of the topics below. Write six sentences. Use the present and past passive, past perfect, or modals of possibility and certainty. Explain what or where it is and why you chose it to write about.

- A special part of the natural environment in your country.
- Your biggest achievement at school this year and your hopes for next year.
- Your favourite place to shop online or in a store.

TEST YOUR MEMORY!

- Say three things you had done before you started school today. Use the past perfect.
- Report three sentences or questions someone said or asked you today.
- Name things you can do with these verbs: *collect, protect, recycle, reuse, save*.
- Give three adjectives that use the affixes *-able* and *-ful*.
- Make five questions using words for education.
- Describe the natural environment where you live.
- Name three things you can see or do when you go shopping offline.
- Make five sentences about your English class. Use phrasal verbs.
- Say three things in the present simple passive.
- Name three things you can see or do when you go shopping online.
- Say two things you are certain will happen and two things you are not sure will happen.
- Make three sentences. Use the past simple passive.

105

PROJECT
UNITS 1–3

TASK
Create a blog post about the best tourist attractions in your region

 work in pairs and produce a blog post.

PREPARE

Step 1 Get ideas
- Look at the tourist photos. Do you know which region of which country they show?
- Which photos belong to each category in the mind map?

Step 2 Choose your recommendations
- Think about your region. Copy the mind map above. Think of ideas for each category.
- Work in pairs. Compare your ideas and choose the five best things to do in your region.

Look! Negotiation
If you and your partner have different opinions about the best things to do, food to try and places to visit in your region, compromise by choosing two personal favourites each, and one thing you both like.

21st Century Skills — Compare cultures
Are there any typical foods in your region? Why are they popular? What do people from other cultures say about them?

Step 3 Do your research
- Ask other students to tell you about their experience of the things you have chosen.

  Have you ever visited Lands End?
  What did you think of it?
  When did you go there?

- Find out more information about the things you have chosen on the internet, or in books and magazines.

PROJECT Units 1-3

▶ DO

Step 4 Plan your blog post
- Decide if your blog post is on a computer or on paper.
- Look at the blog post below.
- Decide what information and photos or drawings you want.

Step 5 Write the text for your blog post
- Write the text for each section of your blog post. Use the **Useful language** box to help you.
- Give your text to another student to check your spelling and punctuation.

Step 6 Create your blog post
- Draw your pictures and print or download your photos and text.
- Put your blog post together.
- Publish your post to the school blog or display it for your class to see.

▶ REFLECT

Step 7 Evaluate the projects
- View or look at all the blog posts. Which looks the best? Which has the best information?
- Say which of the experiences you've already tried. Do you agree with the tourist ratings? Say which experiences you'd like to try and why.

Step 8 Reflect
- Think about your own project. Is there anything you can improve?

> **Useful language**
> Have you ever ...?
> Have you visited ... yet?
> I've just been to ...
> I used to hate ..., but now I love it/them.
> When I was ..., I ....
> It was amazing/interesting/relaxing/exciting.

THE FIVE BEST THINGS TO DO IN SNOWDONIA

Snowdonia is a mountainous region in the north-west of Wales.

1 Climb Mount Snowdon

Have you ever climbed a mountain? Mount Snowdon is the highest mountain in Wales. It's 1,085 metres above sea level.

Carrie
●●●●●
I used to hate walking until I climbed Snowdon. Now I love it! I've just come back from my fourth hiking trip in Snowdonia!

2 Travel on the mountain railway

You can also travel to the top of Mount Snowdon by steam train!

Harry

I've loved steam trains since I was five. I travelled up Mount Snowdon by train last month and I wasn't disappointed! It was amazing!

3 Visit Harlech Castle

King Edward I built this castle in the late thirteenth century.

Lily
●●●●○
I went to Harlech Castle because I'm really interested in medieval history. It's brilliant!

4 Camp in woodlands

Make the most of the countryside and stay outdoors!

Ella

We stayed in a tent near the woods when we were visiting Snowdonia last year. So relaxing!

5 Eat Welsh cakes

Have you tried Welsh cakes yet? They're small, round fruit cakes, cooked in a flat frying pan.

Noah

I was cycling in Snowdonia with my cousins, when we stopped at a traditional café. I tried Welsh cakes for the first time. Yum!

107

PROJECT
UNITS 4-6

TASK
Create a *How to ...* video

I can work in pairs and make a video.

▶ PREPARE

My skills	Things I need	Easy/Difficult to teach
• A card trick	• A pack of playing cards	• Very easy!
•	•	•
•	•	•
•	•	•

Step 1 Get ideas

› Look at the photos from different *How to ...* videos. Which skills do you think the videos are teaching?
› Say what objects or equipment you need to do the activities in each photo. Do you think the activities are easy or difficult to teach?

Step 2 Choose ideas

› Think about your skills or abilities. Copy the table and write a list of things you know how to do in the first column.
› Work in pairs and share your lists. Complete your tables together.
› Decide what you can demonstrate together in a *How to ...* video.

21st Century Skills — Think critically

Do you prefer to read instructions or watch video demonstrations? Why?

Step 3 Do your research

› Ask other students or your family about their experience of learning to do something by watching a video.
› Watch some *How to ...* videos online. How practical and helpful are they?

Look! — Problem solving

Think about the problems that you might have when you make your video. What solutions can you suggest? Can you avoid them?

▶ DO

Step 4 Plan your video

> Look at the storyboard for a *How to ...* video below.
> Think about how many steps you will need to demonstrate your skill or ability.
> Create your own storyboard and draw sketches.

Step 5 Write the script for your video

> Write the script in your storyboard. Use the **Useful language** box to help you.
> Give your script to another student to check your grammar.

Step 6 Create your video

> Find the things you need.
> Practise your video script with your partner.
> Film your video at school or at home.
> Show your *How to ...* video to your class.

▶ REFLECT

Step 7 Evaluate the projects

> Watch your classmates' videos. Which did you enjoy most? Which videos have the most practical advice?
> Tell your group which activities from the videos you'd like to try.

Step 8 Reflect

> Think about your own project. Is there anything you can improve?

Useful language
In this video, we'll be explaining how to ...
First, I'm going to ...
You'll need ...
If you (draw big eyelids), (the eyes) will ...
You should/must/need to ...
You might/could ...
If I were you, I'd ...

PROJECT Units 4–6

1

Sam: In this video, we'll be showing you how to draw different expressions.
Lola: You don't have to be a good artist to draw cartoon faces. It's easy!

2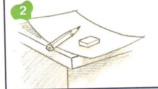

Lola: You'll need some paper and a pencil.
Sam: You might need an eraser, too!

3

Sam: First we're going to draw a tired face. If you draw big eyelids, the eyes will look really tired!

4

Sam: You could draw bags under the eyes, too.
Lola: Oh yes, he looks very tired!

5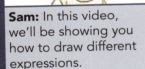

Lola: It's difficult to draw an angry face unless you draw eyebrows. They must go down. If I were you, I'd draw the eyebrows first.

6

Lola: The eyes need to have small pupils. If you draw a wide mouth with teeth like this, the face looks really angry.
Sam: Scary!

7

Sam: My favourite cartoon face is one that is laughing. The mouth should go up like this. The mouth needs to be open, too.

8

Sam: It looks good if you draw the eyes closed. You could add tears of laughter, too!
Lola: That's it for now! In our next video, we'll show you how to draw a frightened face and a sad face.

109

PROJECT
UNITS 7–9

TASK
Create a design for a product made from recycled materials

I can work in pairs and create a design.

▶ PREPARE

 a
 b
 c
 d

Product	Made of	Used for
• greenhouse	• plastic bottles	• growing plants
•	•	•
•	•	•
•	•	•

 e

 f
 g
 h
 i

Step 1 Get ideas
› Look at the photos. What do they all have in common?
› Talk about the things in the photos. What are they made from? What are they used for?

Step 2 Do your research
› Ask your family if you have anything made from recycled materials at home.
› Search ideas for recycled crafts online.

21st Century Skills Get creative
At home, collect materials your family doesn't need anymore. Do these materials give you any good ideas?

Step 3 Choose an idea
› Work in pairs. Think of ideas for things you can make with recycled materials.
› Think of the materials that you will need.
› Copy the table and complete it with your own ideas.
› Look at your ideas together and choose the best one.

Look! Learning through doing
If you're not sure about a design idea, you could try making a prototype or a model of a small part of it.

▶ DO

Step 4 Plan your design

- Look at the ideas for your design.
- Think about how your product is made.
- Plan the diagrams you will need to show how it is made.

Step 5 Write the text for your design

- Read the text for the design below.
- Write about your reasons for choosing your product and how it is made. Use the **Useful language** box to help you.
- Give your text to another student to check your spelling and punctuation.

Step 6 Create and display your design

- Draw and label diagrams to show how your product is made.
- Put your diagrams and text together.
- Display your design for your class to see.

▶ REFLECT

Step 7 Evaluate the projects

- Look at all the designs. Which product is the most attractive or useful? Which product recycles materials well?
- Listen to your classmates' feedback on your product and take notes. Then write a paragraph summarizing what your classmates said.

Step 8 Reflect

- Think about the feedback. Is there anything you can improve?

> **Useful language**
> We came up with an idea for …
> Lots of … are (thrown away).
> Many … aren't (recycled).
> This … is made from …
> First/Then/After that, the bottle is (washed).
> You could use … instead of …
> … said they liked our product.
> One student told us he/she had …

PROJECT Units 7–9

⚡ A MOBILE PHONE CHARGER CASE ⚡

OUR IDEA

Our idea is a mobile phone charger case. It's used to hold your phone when it's charging. We came up with this idea because too many plastic bottles aren't recycled, and lots of old clothes are thrown away. We think this charger case could be really useful!

1. plastic from bottle

3. socket, charger, phone

2. old jeans

glue

HOW IT'S MADE

The case is made from a plastic bottle. It can be a water bottle or a shampoo bottle, for example. First, the bottle is washed and dried, and then cut into a case shape. After that, it's covered with old fabric. The fabric could be from an old shirt or a pair of jeans which are too small. Don't forget to cut a hole for the plug!

FEEDBACK

Ten students told us that they liked our phone charger case.

One student said it was a good idea, because his phone was protected while it was charging.

Another student said she'd just finished a bottle of shampoo and she wanted to try our idea.

Other students in our class asked us what kind of bottle they could use. We explained that they could use any plastic bottle which was big enough for their phone.

Another student asked us whether it was necessary to sew the fabric. We explained that they could use strong glue.

111

LITERATURE
UNITS 1-3

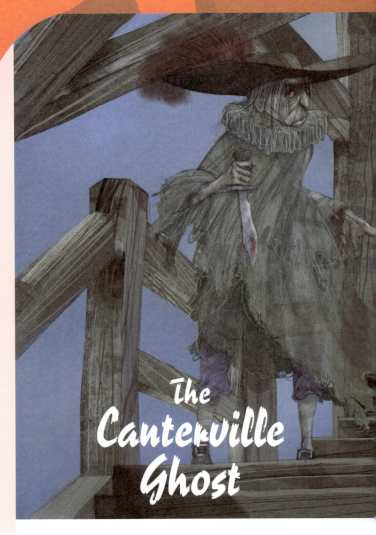

BEFORE YOU READ

1 Work in pairs and answer the questions.
1 Do you think ghosts are real? Why/Why not?
2 Why do you think people are frightened of ghosts?
3 How would you feel if you saw a ghost?

2 Read the outline of *The Canterville Ghost*. Are the sentences true (T) or false (F)? Correct the false sentences.
1 The Otis family are on holiday at Canterville Chase.
2 Lord Canterville's family were too frightened to live in the house any more.
3 Mr Otis isn't frightened of the ghost when he meets him one night.
4 When the twins meet the ghost they run away.
5 The ghost is happy that no one is frightened of him.

OUTLINE — **The Canterville Ghost**

Mr and Mrs Otis and their four children, Washington, Virginia and the twin boys are a rich American family. They have bought Canterville Chase, an old English country house, from Lord Canterville. He decided to sell the house because of a terrible ghost who was frightening his family. But Mr Otis isn't frightened – he doesn't believe in ghosts.

Soon after they move in, Mr Otis wakes up to the sound of the ghost in the middle of the night. The ghost is an old man with red eyes, long, dirty hair and very old clothes. But Mr Otis isn't frightened of him. Later that evening, the ghost meets the twins, who throw something at him. Now the ghost is annoyed that no one is frightened of him and thinks of a plan to frighten them.

READ

3 🔊 L1 Look at the picture. Read and listen to the extract from *The Canterville Ghost* and answer the questions.
1 Who is the figure in the picture?
2 What is he planning to do?
3 Does his plan work?

The Ghostly Plan

When he felt better, he decided to try again to frighten the American family. This time, he made very careful preparations.

First, he decided what clothes to wear. He chose a large hat with a red feather. Then he put a white shroud round himself. Finally, he picked up a large, bloodstained knife. In the evening a violent storm broke. A strong wind blew noisily through the old house. The ghost was pleased. It was just the kind of weather he loved.

He went through his plan of action. 'I will go to Washington Otis's room first and make noises at the foot of his bed. Then I will push the knife into myself three times. Slow, sad music will play. When the young man is helpless with terror, I will go to the parents' room. I will put a thin, ice-cold hand on Mrs Otis's head and say awful things in a low, frightening voice to Mr Otis.' The ghost was not quite so certain about his plans for Virginia. She was gentle and pretty, and she had never tried to hurt him. 'A few alarming noises from inside the cupboard in her room will be enough,' he thought.

But he certainly intended to frighten the terrible twins. 'First, I will sit on them heavily so that they cannot breathe. Then I will appear in the form of a dead body, lit by a horrible green light …'

At half past ten, he heard the family going to bed. For some time there were screams of laughter from the twins' room. But at a quarter past eleven all was quiet and at midnight, the ghost left his room. A barn owl

LITERATURE
Units 1–3

4 Read the extract again. Complete the sentences with the words in the box. There are two extra words.

| asleep | bird | crying | figure | knife |
| laughter | room | storm |

1 The ghost got dressed up and carried a ... with him to scare the family.
2 It was very windy and there was a terrible ... .
3 After the Otis family went to bed the ghost heard ... in the twins' room.
4 By 11.15 p.m. the family was ... .
5 Before he reached Washington's room, the ghost was frightened by a strange ... .
6 He ran back to his ... and stayed there until the next day.

5 **Word Power** Find the negative adjectives in the text that describe these things. How many more negative adjectives can you think of?

1 a ... voice
2 the ... twins
3 a ... green light
4 a ... smile
5 a ... figure

6 🔊 L2 Look at the picture and listen to the next part of the story. Answer the questions.

'The Only True and Original Otis Ghost! Take care! All other ghosts are false.'

1 What did the ghost decide to do in the morning?
2 Why did the ghost have a terrible shock when he tried to lift the other ghost up?
3 What was the other ghost made from?
4 Why did he become angry after reading the notice?
5 What did the ghost promise to do when the cock crowed twice?
6 What time did the ghost go back to his room?

called softly from a tree outside the window. The wind cried like a lost child through the empty rooms of the house. But the Otis family slept peacefully, unconscious of the coming danger.

The ghost moved quietly through the darkness of the sleeping house. A cruel smile touched his dry, old mouth. He held his bloody knife high in the air. He felt so powerful! He was beginning to enjoy himself.

Still smiling, he turned the corner to reach Washington's room. He stopped with a shout of terror! Directly in front of him stood a terrible, ghostly figure. It was like a madman's worst dream. The large, round head was white and hairless. The fat face was smiling horribly. A strange red fire lit up its eyes and mouth. The awful figure was wearing a white shroud, very like his own. There was a notice on the cloth in strange, old writing. In its right hand, the figure held a large, sharp knife.

The Canterville ghost had never before seen anything like this! He was extremely frightened. He gave the awful thing one last look. Then he ran back to his own room, where he hid under the bed until morning.

Glossary
shroud a cloth, or loose clothing
bloodstained with marks of blood
helpless not able to help yourself
cruel extremely unkind

Extract from **Richmond Readers**: *The Canterville Ghost and Other Stories* by Oscar Wilde

▶ REFLECT

7 **GET CREATIVE** Work in groups. Imagine you are the Otis family. What do you think you could do to get the ghost to leave the house forever? Discuss in groups and present a plan to the class.

113

LITERATURE
UNITS 4–6

Dr Jekyll & Mr Hyde

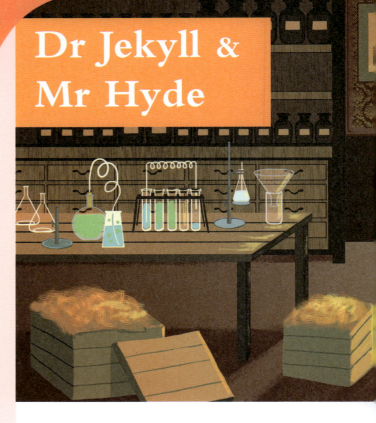

BEFORE YOU READ

1 Work in pairs and answer the questions.
1 What does a lawyer do?
2 How did the police solve crimes in the nineteenth century? How do they do it today?

2 Read the outline of *Dr Jekyll & Mr Hyde*. Complete the sentences.
1 Mr Utterson is … about his friend Dr Jekyll.
2 Dr Jekyll wants Mr Hyde to have all his … if he dies.
3 Mr Hyde has a … to a room in Dr Jekyll's house.
4 Mr Hyde uses a … that belongs to Dr Jekyll to kill Sir Danvers Carew late one night.
5 Dr Jekyll shows Mr Utterson a … from Mr Hyde.

OUTLINE — Dr Jekyll & Mr Hyde

Mr Utterson is a lawyer in nineteenth century London. He is worried about his close friend Dr Henry Jekyll, a kind and clever scientist. Mr Utterson has a will (a document which says what to do with someone's money and possessions when they die) from Dr Jekyll. It says that when Dr Jekyll dies, Mr Utterson must give all his money to a strange and nasty young man called Edward Hyde. Mr Utterson also knows that Mr Hyde has a key to an old laboratory in Dr Jekyll's house. When Mr Utterson visits the doctor, Dr Jekyll makes him promise to take care of Mr Hyde if anything happens to him. But Mr Utterson thinks that Dr Jekyll is in trouble with Mr Hyde.

A year later, Mr Hyde kills an old man called Sir Danvers Carew in the street late at night. The walking stick he uses for the murder belongs to Dr Jekyll. Mr Utterson visits Dr Jekyll again to warn him about Mr Hyde. Dr Jekyll tells him he is not worried by the young man and shows him a letter that Mr Hyde has written to him.

READ

3 🔊 L3 Look at the picture. Read and listen to the extract from *Dr Jekyll & Mr Hyde* and answer the questions.
1 Who are the two people in the picture?
2 What are they looking at? What is important about it?
3 How do you think they feel? Why?

The Letter

The writing on the letter was strange. It said:

> *Thank you for a thousand acts of kindness. You need not be afraid for me. I have a safe and dependable way of escaping.*
>
> *Edward Hyde*

Mr Utterson felt a little better after reading it. 'Do you have the envelope?' he asked.

'I burnt it,' Dr Jekyll replied. 'But the letter was not posted. Somebody brought it to the house.'

'Shall I keep this?' Mr Utterson asked.

'I will leave the decision to you,' Dr Jekyll replied.

'I will consider all this,' Mr Utterson said. 'But I have one more question. Was it Hyde who told you what to say in your will about disappearing?'

For a moment, it looked as though Dr Jekyll was going to faint. Then he quietly said, 'Yes.'

'I knew it!' Mr Utterson cried. 'He planned to murder you! You were lucky to escape!'

'I have learned a lesson, Utterson,' Dr Jekyll said. 'Oh, what a lesson I have learned!' And he covered his face with his hands.

On his way out of the house, Mr Utterson stopped to speak to Poole.

'A letter was delivered today,' he said. 'Who brought it, Poole? What did he look like?'

'A letter, Sir?' Poole said. 'No letter was delivered by hand today. The only letters that came were those that came through the post.'

LITERATURE
Units 4–6

All Mr Utterson's fears returned as he left the house. 'Did the letter come through the laboratory door?' he wondered. 'Or was it written in the upstairs room of the laboratory? If it was, I must be extremely careful what I do.'

Mr Utterson walked home through the streets. Newspaper boys were shouting, 'Murder! Murder! Sir Danvers Carew murdered! Read all about it!' as he walked by them.

A good friend and client was dead. Was that death about to hurt the good reputation of another? He would have to be careful to make the right decision. 'For the first time for many years,' thought Mr Utterson, 'I need some advice.'

Soon after, he was sitting beside his fireplace with Mr Guest, the head clerk from Mr Utterson's office. A bottle of good wine stood on the table between them. Outside, the fog still covered the city, but the fire made the room warm and bright.

Mr Utterson kept very few secrets from Guest, and Guest had often gone to Dr Jekyll's house on business. He knew Poole and he must also know about Mr Hyde. Was it a good idea to let him see the letter? Mr Utterson thought that it was. He knew that Guest was a student of handwriting and a man able to give good advice.

Glossary
escape to get free from something
faint become unconscious suddenly
to be delivered to take letters or parcels to people's houses
murder the crime of killing a person

Extract from **Richmond Readers**: *Dr Jekyll & Mr Hyde* by Robert Louis Stevenson

4 Read the extract again and choose the correct answer.
1 After reading the letter, Mr Utterson …
 a wanted to burn it.
 b didn't feel as bad as before.
2 Mr Utterson believed that …
 a Mr Hyde planned to kill Dr Jekyll so he could have all his money.
 b Mr Hyde wanted to escape.
3 Dr Jekyll's servant, Poole, told Mr Utterson that …
 a a number of letters were delivered by hand.
 b some letters came in the post but none came by hand.
4 Mr Utterson visited his colleague, Mr Guest …
 a to ask him for help.
 b to tell him the news about Sir Danvers Carew.
5 Mr Utterson decided to show Mr Guest …
 a the newspaper story.
 b the letter from Edward Hyde.

5 **Word Power** Complete the three compound nouns from the text. Can you think of five more compound nouns for things you use at home?
1 …paper 2 fire… 3 hand…

6 🔊 **L4** Listen to the next part of the story. Put the events in order from 1–6.
a … Mr Utterson cannot understand why Dr Jekyll wrote a letter for the murderer.
b … Mr Utterson shows Mr Guest the letter from the murderer.
c … Mr Utterson locks the note in a safe.
d … Mr Guest believes the handwriting on the note and the letter are very similar.
e … A servant brings Mr Utterson a note from Dr Jekyll.
f … Mr Guest compares the handwriting on the note from Dr Jekyll with the letter from the murderer.

▶ REFLECT

7 💭 **THINK CRITICALLY** Work in pairs. Read these facts from the story and answer the questions.
1 Why do you think Dr Jekyll agreed to give Mr Hyde all his money when he dies?
2 How do you think Dr Jekyll received the letter from Mr Hyde?
3 Why do you think Dr Jekyll and Mr Hyde's handwriting is so similar?

> Mr Hyde told Dr Jekyll to give him all his money in his will.
>
> The letter from Mr Hyde to Dr Jekyll was not delivered by hand or by post.
>
> The handwriting on the letter from Mr Hyde was very similar to Dr Jekyll's handwriting.

LITERATURE
UNITS 7–9

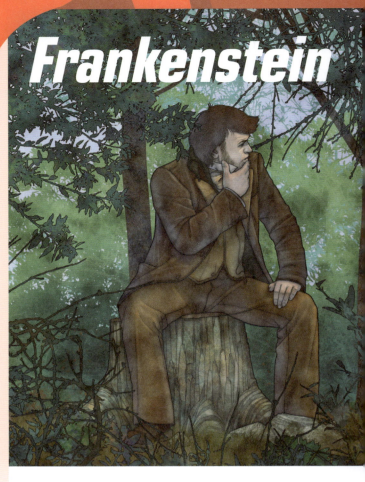

▶ BEFORE YOU READ

1 Work in pairs and answer the questions.
1 What do you know about the story, *Frankenstein*?
2 Who was Frankenstein?
3 What did he do?

2 Read the outline of *Frankenstein*. Put the events in order from 1–7.
a Victor's brother is killed.
b Victor goes to study at university.
c Victor creates a monster.
d Victor learns how to create life.
e Victor meets the monster again.
f Victor's mother dies.
g The monster runs away.

OUTLINE — Frankenstein

Victor Frankenstein is an ambitious student in eighteenth-century Geneva. When he is seventeen, his mother dies after a short illness. Soon after this, Victor goes to university in Ingolstadt. He leaves his family and best friend behind and spends all his time studying chemistry. He becomes very interested in life and death and after many months of study, he discovers how to create life. He spends the next two years creating a giant human, a monster, and gives it life.

Victor becomes very ill and the monster escapes from the laboratory. Some time later, Victor's younger brother William is murdered. Victor is sure that the monster is the killer. He meets the monster again living in the mountains. The monster admits to killing William and tells Victor he is very unhappy and lonely. He says that after he left the laboratory, he tried to make friends with a family called the De Laceys, but they rejected him because he was so ugly. He tells Victor that all he wants is a female friend, a companion, someone like him.

▶ READ

3 🔊 L5 Look at the picture. Read and listen to the extract from *Frankenstein* and answer the questions.
1 Where are Victor and the monster?
2 What is the monster asking?
3 How do you think they are both feeling?
4 What agreement do they make?

A Gentleman's Agreement

After the monster had finished speaking, he waited for me to reply. But I was too shocked to answer immediately.

'You must make a female for me,' he repeated. 'I demand it and you cannot say "no".'

'I will not do it,' I said at last. 'Nothing will ever make me agree. Shall I make another thing like you? Together, you might destroy the world.'

'I am evil only because I am unhappy,' the monster said. 'Why must I love humans more than they love me? If they are kind to me, I will be friendly. But that won't happen. So, if people cannot love me, I will give them reasons to fear me!'

A horrible, angry light burned in his eyes for a moment. When he became calmer, he continued. 'I am being reasonable, Frankenstein. Just make me happy. Let me feel thankful to you for one kind action.'

His words touched my heart. He had made a good argument. I could see that he was a sensitive creature. 'I must give him a little happiness if I can,' I thought.

He saw my feelings change. 'If you agree, Frankenstein, no humans will ever see us again,' he said. 'We will go to the wildest parts of South America. We will live on the fruits of the earth. We will sleep on dry leaves. The sun will keep us warm.'

'You promise to live peacefully,' I said. 'But you have already done bad things. Having a female will give you twice as much power.'

116

LITERATURE
Units 7-9

4 Read the extract again and choose the correct answer.
1. At first, Frankenstein refuses to make a female ...
   a because he doesn't know how to.
   b because he is worried they will be dangerous.
2. The monster says he is bad because ...
   a people do not show him any love.
   b he doesn't know how to be good.
3. Frankenstein agrees to help the monster because ...
   a he would like to continue his work.
   b he can see that he has feelings.
4. The monster promises Frankenstein that if he helps him ...
   a he will stay and help Frankenstein.
   b he will leave the country forever.
5. The monster tells Frankenstein that ...
   a he will return when Frankenstein has completed the female monster.
   b he won't watch him while he is working.
6. After the meeting, Frankenstein feels ...
   a pleased with the agreement.
   b worried for his family.

5 A **Word Power** Match the adverbs in blue in the text with the meanings.
1. without doubt
2. happening straight away
3. quietly or calmly

B Find adjectives in the extract. Make adverbs from them.

6 🔊 **L6** Listen to the next part of the story. Choose the correct answers.
1. Frankenstein was worried that the female monster might have *children / problems*.
2. While Frankenstein was working, the monster appeared *during the day / at night*.
3. Frankenstein picked up the female monster and *broke / held* it.
4. The monster became very *angry / sad* after this.
5. Frankenstein told the monster to *go away / stay*.
6. The monster told Frankenstein that he would live in *peace / fear*.

▶ REFLECT

7 💬 **THINK CRITICALLY** Work in groups. Discuss these questions about Victor and the monster.
1. Were you frightened of the monster at the end?
2. Can you understand his anger and pain?
3. Have your feelings towards the monster changed during the story? How and why?
4. How do you think Victor is feeling at the end of the story?
5. Was Victor right to destroy the monster's companion? What would you do?

'I am serious, Frankenstein,' the monster replied. 'If there is no love in my life, hate will fill my heart instead. But the love of another creature will take away the cause of my crimes.'

I paused to think about his arguments. He had certainly shown good qualities at the beginning of his life. His kind feelings had been destroyed by his unhappy experience with the De Lacey family. I must not forget that he had great power. 'If I don't help him, he will be a danger to all human life,' I thought. I had to do what he asked.

'I agree to your demand,' I said. 'But you and the female must leave Europe forever.'

'After you have done this for me, you will never see me again. This is my promise, Frankenstein,' he said. 'Remember, I shall watch you during your work. When you are ready, I shall appear again.'

When I returned home, my wild look alarmed my family. But I could not answer their questions. In fact, I did not speak to them at all. I felt as if I were no longer part of their community and could never again enjoy their company. My urgent duty now was to save them from the monster. Nothing else in life mattered.

> **Glossary**
> **demand** to ask for something in a firm way
> **evil** morally bad
> **reasonable** fair, practical and sensible
> **duty** something you have to do

Extract from **Richmond Readers**: *Frankenstein* by Mary Shelley

EXAM PRACTICE UNIT 1

READING
Multiple matching

> **Look!** **About the task**
>
> In this reading task, you read descriptions of different people and match them with short texts on a particular topic. There are more short texts than you need.

> **Useful strategies**
> - Read the descriptions of the people and underline any important words and phrases.
> - Then read the short texts and look for words and phrases that mean the same thing.
> - Choose the text that matches all the information in each person's description, not just a word or phrase.

1 Read about Maria and find the important information.

> Maria loves music and would love to see a film about the adventures of some well-known musicians on tour. She likes pretending she's a pop star and she doesn't want to see anything too serious.

2 Now read the film description below. Find any words and phrases that match the words you underlined in Exercise 1.

INSIDE

This is the perfect film if you're interested in celebrities! It looks at life for members of Boom – the world's most famous pop band – as they travel through the USA. The film has plenty of comedy moments and fans are encouraged to dress up like Boom members to watch the film.

OUR VERDICT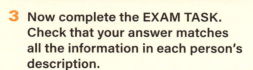

3 Now complete the EXAM TASK. Check that your answer matches all the information in each person's description.

EXAM TASK

For each question, choose the correct answer.
The people below all want to find a film to watch this weekend at their local cinema. Read the five film reviews and decide which film would be the most suitable for the following people.

1 Jilani loves films that are set in different locations around the world. He'd like to watch an adventure film and he's very interested in animals, in particular, jungle animals.

2 Shani wants to see a film where the people are in dangerous environments. She prefers watching comedy films and likes seeing people while they're at work.

3 Ulrika loves watching nature films. It's not important to her whether the actors are famous, but she enjoys seeing films that are part of a series.

FILM REVIEWS   REVIEWS ARTICLES BLOG

A BUSY LIVES

This documentary film is a must see for all animal-lovers out there! You'll learn about the lives of animals in some of Africa's most historical and famous nature parks, and those who work with them, too. There aren't many laughs and it's slightly different from the book, *Busy Lives*, but you'll still learn loads!

B DESERT

If you've seen the first *Desert* movie, the characters in this one will be familiar to you. Set in the Sahara Desert, it follows the travels of three scientists as they learn all about life there. It has some less well-known actors, but that doesn't make it boring.

C THE A GAME

The A Game is so exciting that you'll be on the edge of your seat. Funny in places, there's plenty of action as the team of scientists learn about the creatures they meet doing their research, while travelling through the rainforests of South America.

D THE GILROYS

The prize-winning director of this film is well known for his amazing adventure movies. Sure to make you laugh and with lots of our top film stars, his latest film's set in the jungle, where the Gilroy family find themselves in danger as they make their way through the jungle and avoid unknown animals!

E DEEP BLUE

With a cast full of famous actors, *Deep Blue* is one of this year's funniest films. The characters have many adventures as they do their jobs as a team of divers in difficult conditions deep under water. It has a serious side too, though – they're not safe, as they swim with lots of frightening sharks!

EXAM PRACTICE
UNIT 2

LISTENING
Multiple choice

Look! About the task

In this listening task, you will hear some short dialogues or messages and answer some multiple-choice questions. For each question, you must choose the correct picture to answer the question. You hear each dialogue twice.

Useful strategies

- Before listening, read the questions and look at the three pictures.
- Think about the kind of words you are going to hear.
- You'll hear something about <u>all</u> the pictures for each question. Listen for the whole meaning, not just individual words.

1 Work in pairs. Look at the pictures in EXAM TASK question 1. Think of two or three words you might hear for each picture.

2 Now do the same for the pictures in questions 2–5. Discuss your answers with your partner.

3 🔊 **E2.1** Look at EXAM TASK question 1. Read and listen to the dialogue. Which is the correct answer? Why?

Girl: Have you ever been to London?

Boy: Yeah, I went there with my parents last summer. It was totally awesome!

Girl: Did you buy anything interesting when you were there?

Boy: Well, I almost bought a really cool T-shirt, but then I decided I had enough of those from all the other places I've been to! I got a baseball cap instead. My sister got this really funny book of British jokes ... hang on ... let me go and get it for you.

Girl: OK!

4 Now complete the EXAM TASK.

EXAM TASK

🔊 **E2.2** For each question there are three pictures and a short recording. Choose the correct picture A, B or C.

1 Which souvenir did the boy buy in London?

A   B   C

2 How will the boy travel to the birthday party today?

A   B   C

3 What did the girl do first on her holiday?

A   B   C

4 Where is the woman now?

A   B   C

5 Which photo does the girl like best?

A   B   C

EXAM PRACTICE UNIT 3

SPEAKING
Conversation

> **Look!** About the task
>
> In this speaking task, the examiner asks you questions about two topics. There are six possible topics. You must also ask the examiner a question.

Useful strategies

- Listen carefully to the question to see which tense the examiner uses.
- Don't worry if you make a mistake while you are speaking – if you can, correct it and continue speaking.
- If you didn't understand the question, ask the examiner to repeat it.

1 Work with a partner. Think of questions the examiner could ask you about these topics:

- festivals / special occasions
  Where do you usually ...?
  Are you going to ...?
- recent personal events
  When did you last ...?
  Have you ever ...?

2 ◉ **E3.1** Read the following four questions and choose the best answer to each. Say why it is the correct answer. Listen and check.

1. How do you usually celebrate your birthday?
   a   I always have a party at home. All my friends come round.
   b   I'll have a party at home. I'll invite lots of friends!
2. When was your last holiday?
   a   I've already had one.
   b   It was in August last year.
3. What are you going to do at the weekend?
   a   I'm going to visit my grandparents. They live in a small town not far from my home.
   b   Nothing special. I was at home. I did my homework and watched some TV.
4. Have you ever been to a festival in another country?
   a   Yes, I'd really love to do that one day.
   b   Yes, and it was fantastic.

3 ◉ **E3.2** Listen to two conversations and complete the table. Which conversation is better? Why?

The student ...	A	B
1 answers the questions correctly.		
2 gives detailed answers.		
3 asks the examiner a question.		

4 ◉ **E3.3** Now listen to how a student answers the questions in the EXAM TASK.

5 Work in pairs. Complete the EXAM TASK.

EXAM TASK

Take turns asking each other questions 1–6. Add some questions of your own.

1. What did you do last weekend?
2. When did you last speak to your friends?
3. What will you do for your next birthday?
4. Who were you with on your last holiday?
5. What is the most popular festival in your country?
6. Do people wear special clothes for this festival?

EXAM PRACTICE
UNIT 4

LISTENING
Interview

> **Look!** About the task
>
> In this listening task, you will hear an interview and answer six multiple-choice questions. Some questions will be about facts and details, others will be about feelings or opinions. You hear each dialogue twice.

> **Useful strategies**
> - Before listening, read all the instructions and questions to get an idea of the topic.
> - For each question, listen for the whole meaning, not just individual words.
> - The first time you listen, choose an answer. Then listen again and check.

1 Look at the EXAM TASK and questions 1–6. What do you think the interview is about?

2 Look again at question 1 of the EXAM TASK. Read the first part of the interview below. Find the important words.

> I've loved cooking since I was a child, and when I brought some food into school once for an end-of-year party, my mates loved it. Some of them asked me to teach them to cook. My Maths teacher even ordered some food from me! Anyway, when I told Mum and Dad, they said I should make a business out of it.

3 🔊 E4.1 Listen to question 1 of the EXAM TASK and look at the words you found in Exercise 2. Which words give you the correct answer? Why?

4 🔊 E4.2 Now listen and complete questions 2–6 of the EXAM TASK.

EXAM TASK

For each question, choose the correct answer.
You will hear an interview with a young woman called Carly Hall, who has a catering business.

1 Why did Carly decide to start her catering business?
   a Her parents encouraged her to start a company.
   b Her teacher thought she was good at business.
   c Her friends told her they loved her food.
2 What was Carly's biggest challenge when she started her business?
   a organizing her time
   b managing complaints
   c inventing new recipes
3 What does Carly think about cooking meat?
   a It allows her to be creative.
   b It requires more skill than fish.
   c It is easier to work with than people think.
4 In order to improve her business, Carly believes she should
   a spend more money on advertising.
   b be more original with her cooking.
   c develop more confidence in herself.
5 What does Carly plan to do in the future?
   a have her own restaurant
   b teach young people
   c write a book
6 Carly advises people who want to start a catering business
   a to be sensible.
   b to be patient.
   c to be positive.

121

EXAM PRACTICE
UNIT 5

LISTENING
Sentence completion

> **Look!** **About the task**
>
> In this listening task, you will hear someone talking about a topic and complete some sentences. You fill each gap with a word or short noun phrase. You hear each dialogue twice.

Useful strategies

- Read the sentences carefully before you listen and think about what kind of information you need to complete the gaps (e.g. a noun, number, place, date, price).
- Remember that you will hear some information which sounds as if it could fit the gap, but is <u>not</u> correct.
- The words you write will be the same as the words you hear on the recording.

1 You will hear Petra talking about learning Spanish. For each gap 1–3, choose which kind of word is needed from options a–c below.

Petra's Spanish course

Last year, Petra spent three weeks in ¹ ... learning Spanish.

The woman Petra stayed with is a ² ... .

Each day, Petra had lessons for ³ ... hours.

---

a   a noun or noun phrase
b   a number
c   a place

2 Work in pairs. Before you listen, write two or three possible words for each gap. Discuss with your partner.

3 🔊 **E5.1** Now listen to Petra. Complete each sentence with the correct word.

4 Work in pairs. Compare your answers. Did you choose the right words in Exercise 2?

5 Now complete the EXAM TASK.

EXAM TASK

🔊 **E5.2** You will hear a college student called Alfie telling his classmates about a language course he has done. For each question, complete the missing information.

Alfie's Greek course

Alfie spent ¹ ... weeks in Athens learning Greek.

Alfie didn't have to attend lessons in the ² ... .

During the course, Alfie had some problems with ³ ... .

Alfie thought the ⁴ ... the teachers gave was very interesting.

The most enjoyable day for Alfie was a visit to ⁵ ... .

Now, Alfie plans to use ⁶ ... to improve his Greek.

EXAM PRACTICE
UNIT 6

WRITING
A story

Look! About the task

In this writing task, you write a short story. You are given the first sentence of the story. You then finish it with your own ideas, using the correct number of words.

Useful strategies

- Before writing, read the question carefully, checking who the main character is.
- Then plan your story, organizing it into paragraphs.
- Include a range of language in your story, e.g. different verb tenses, modal verbs, adjectives and adverbs. Use connectives to join sentences together.

1 Read the example exam task below and answer the questions.

> Your English teacher has asked you to write a story.
>
> Write your answer in about **100** words.
>
> Your story must begin with this sentence:
>
> *I felt excited as I sat down with my friends on the train.*
>
> Write your **story**.

1. How many words do you need to write?
2. Who is the main character in the story?
3. Where are the characters?
4. How do they feel?

2 Read the exam task in Exercise 1 again. Then read Paola's and Vincenzo's answers below. Complete the table for each story.

Paola

1 School football final. 2 At the stadium – no seats! 3 After the match.

Story

I felt excited as I sat down with my friends on the train. Maria, Roberto and I were going to support our friend Gianni and our school football team. The team were taking part in the football final because they'd beaten all the other teams.

We arrived at the stadium before eleven, but we couldn't find anywhere to sit because it was so crowded. We had to stand, but we didn't mind that. The other team were terrible. However, Gianni played brilliantly and scored two goals! Our team won!

After the match, we went for a delicious pizza with Gianni and the others. It was such a fantastic day!

(109 words)

Vincenzo

A football match

Story

I felt excited as I sat down with my friends on the train. Me and Carlos went to football match. My friend Marco play in a match in stadium. The stadium was busy. We have to standing. That is OK. Marco is very brilliant player and he was scoring one goal. Our team was winning the match. We all went to eat pizza. It was a very fantastic day.

(69 words)

The story ...	Paola	Vincenzo
1 has a plan.		
2 has the correct main character (I).		
3 is organized into different paragraphs.		-
4 includes more different tenses.		
5 includes adjectives and adverbs.		
6 uses connectors to join sentences.		
7 has enough words.		
8 has incorrect language.		

3 Now complete the EXAM TASK. Write a plan first. Check your work carefully to make sure you have answered all the questions and correct any mistakes.

EXAM TASK

Your English teacher has asked you to write a story. Write your answer in about **100** words. Your story must begin with this sentence:

Alex walked down the stairs and opened the door nervously.

Write your **story**.

EXAM PRACTICE
UNIT 7

READING
Multiple-choice cloze

Look! About the task

In this reading task, you complete a short text with some words missing. You must choose the correct answer from four similar words to complete each gap.

Useful strategies
- Read the text once to get an idea of the topic.
- Think about the kind of word you need for each gap. Does it fit the meaning of the whole sentence?
- After completing the text, read it again to check it makes sense.

1 Read this short text. What is it about?

Forests cover 30% of the Earth's ¹… and 20% of the world's oxygen is ²… in the Amazon rainforest. ³…, we are losing a lot of the world's forests ⁴… many trees are ⁵… to produce furniture and paper. It is estimated that in 100 years, there will be ⁶… rainforests left.

2 Read the text in Exercise 1 again. Write down two possible words to complete each gap. Compare your answers with a partner.

3 Work in pairs. Read the text about how to reduce waste. Look at the gaps. Which word best fills each gap? Why?

You can reuse materials ¹… than throwing them away. For example, you can use a plastic water bottle again and again. Also, you can ²… on materials to other people who could use them, too! Remember, one man's rubbish is ³… man's treasure!

1	a more	b before	c rather	d instead
2	a spend	b pass	c give	d take
3	a other	b some	c the	d another

4 Now complete the EXAM TASK.

EXAM TASK

For each question, choose the correct answer.

Elephants

Elephants are very interesting animals that live in parts of Africa and Asia. The African Elephant is ¹… into two species, the African Forest Elephant and the African Bush Elephant. Female elephants are called cows, and they spend their ²… lives living in large groups called herds. Male elephants leave their herds at ³… thirteen years old. On average, both male and female elephants live until around 70 years old, which is ⁴… to humans.

Many people know that elephants have excellent memories. ⁵…, what's less well known is that elephants have a sense of humour – they love playing ⁶… on people!

1	a shared	b divided	c broken	d torn
2	a many	b full	c whole	d total
3	a definitely	b absolutely	c completely	d approximately
4	a similar	b regular	c same	d familiar
5	a Since	b Even	c Despite	d However
6	a jokes	b comedy	c fun	d entertainment

124

EXAM PRACTICE
UNIT 8

SPEAKING
Picture description

Look! **About the task**

In this speaking task, you describe a photograph. The examiner tells you the topic of the photograph but doesn't ask you any questions. You must describe the photo in detail for about one minute.

Useful strategies

- Imagine you are describing the photo to someone who can't see it. Don't worry about the words you don't know – use the words you do know.
- Give facts about what you can see but also give your opinion.
- Keep talking until the examiner stops you.

1 Work in pairs. Look at the photo below and think about what kind of things you could describe: where they are, what they are doing, etc.

2 Now describe the photo in more detail. Are the sentences true (T) or false (F)? Correct the false sentences.
1. Two boys and a girl are sitting at a table.
2. They are in a classroom.
3. They are having lunch.
4. There are some colourful chairs next to the tables.
5. There are some exercise books on the table.

3 Which of the sentences below give facts? Which give opinions? Write F (facts) or O (opinions).
1. They could be doing homework or a project.
2. They are sitting at a table.
3. They might be in a café.
4. They are using laptops.
5. They look like students.
6. Maybe they're doing schoolwork.

4 🔊 E8.1 Listen to Sophia describing the picture. Which of the following does Sophia do? Write Y (yes) and N (no).
1. Says where the people in the photo are.
2. Says how many people there are.
3. Describes what is happening.
4. Talks about why the people might be happy.
5. Says what might be happening?

5 🔊 E8.2 Now listen to Martin describing the same photo. Which of the following is he sure about and which is he not sure about? Complete the table.

	Sure	Not sure
1 There are two boys and a girl.		
2 They're students.		
3 They're sixteen years old.		
4 The boy on the right is wearing a grey T-shirt.		
5 They're friends.		
6 There's a blue folder on the table.		
7 They're in a café.		

6 In pairs, complete the EXAM TASK. Take turns to describe one of the photos each.

EXAM TASK

I'm going to give you a photograph of students on a school trip.

Here's your photograph. Please tell me what you can see in your photograph.

EXAM PRACTICE UNIT 9

READING Short texts

> **Look!** **About the task**
>
> In this reading task, you read some short texts (an advertisement, a note, a text message or a notice). You choose the answer that best describes the purpose of the text from three options.

Useful strategies

- Read the whole text once to get an idea of the topic.
- Then read the text again, underlining the important words.
- Read all three options carefully. Choose the option that matches the main purpose of the notice, not just because it matches a word.

1 Read the text below. What is its purpose? Choose a, b or c.

ALL CYCLISTS

Bicycles which are left here may be removed. Please leave bicycles in the bike park behind the school.

a to warn cyclists that their bicycles could be stolen
b to apologize to cyclists for taking their bicycles away
c to inform cyclists where they should put their bicycles

2 Now read texts 1–4 in the EXAM TASK. Match one of the descriptions below with each text. Which words in the text helped you to decide?

a selling something
b making a suggestion
c informing
d giving an instruction

3 Read EXAM TASK question 1. Which option matches the whole meaning of the text? Why?

4 Now complete the rest of the EXAM TASK.

EXAM TASK

For each question, choose the correct answer.

1

Kazumi,

I just want to let you know the traffic's awful – but I hope I'll get there by 2 p.m. Luckily, we've already had our lunch, but can you get some coffee for us?

Hideki

Why is Hideki texting?
a to tell his friend that he will do him a favour
b to inform his friend that he may not be on time
c to remind his friend that they have a plan together

2

Due to recent damage done to the school roof during the storm, the front entrance is not considered safe to use.

Until further notice, please use the side door on Victoria St or the back entrance.

a Students should wait for updates about how safe one entrance is.
b All visitors to the building should only use one entrance for now.
c The bad weather is expected to continue for some time.

3

Megan,

I'm working late tonight so unfortunately I won't be home for dinner. Why don't you and your sister order a Chinese takeaway? I've left some money on your desk. I'll eat at work.

Dad

a Megan should buy something for her father's dinner.
b Megan's father has bought food for her to eat.
c Megan can eat before her father comes back home.

4

FOR SALE

Latest model laptop and black bag.
Some damage to both screen and bag.

Call Duane after 7 p.m. – 08944 31465

a The items Duane's selling aren't in perfect condition.
b You can contact Duane any time you like.
c Duane's laptop is an old-fashioned one.

LANGUAGE SUMMARY
UNIT 1

GRAMMAR
used to

Affirmative	Negative
I **used to** live in Madrid.	I **didn't use to** be interested in music.
You **used to** be shy.	We **didn't use to** watch horror films.
She **used to** get very excited on her birthday.	They **didn't use to** watch TV.
Questions	**Short answers**
Did you **use to** share a room?	Yes, I **did**. / No, I **didn't**.
Did he **use to** live near here?	Yes, he **did**. / No, he **didn't**.
Did they **use to** go to school here?	Yes, they **did**. / No, they **didn't**.

Rules

We use *used to* to talk about past habits and old routines.

We use *used to* when the state or action lasted for some time or happened repeatedly.

We use the infinitive *use* (not *used*) in negative sentences and questions.

Past simple vs past continuous

Past simple	Past continuous
I **found** my old camera **while** I **was tidying** my room.	
The phone **rang while** I **was doing** my homework.	
Past continuous	**Past simple**
While I **was tidying** my room, I **found** my old camera.	
While I **was doing** my homework, the phone **rang**.	
Past continuous	**Past simple**
I **was tidying** my room **when** I **found** my old camera.	
I **was doing** my homework **when** the phone **rang**.	

Rules

We often use the past simple and past continuous tenses in the same sentence.

We use the past simple to describe the completed action.

We use the past continuous to describe the action that was in progress.

We use *while* before the past continuous.

We use *when* before the past simple.

VOCABULARY
-ed and -ing adjectives

amazed / amazing
amused / amusing
annoyed / annoying
bored / boring
confused / confusing
disappointed / disappointing
embarrassed / embarrassing
excited / exciting
frightened / frightening
interested / interesting
relaxed / relaxing
surprised / surprising
tired / tiring

Arts and entertainment

audience
carnival
costume
entertainer
entertainment
event
exhibition
fair
festival
parade
performance
performer
reporter
workshop

SPEAKING
Talking about a past event

How was your weekend/holiday?
How did you find out/hear about it?
What was it like?
Who did you go with?
What did you like most about it?
It was amazing/brilliant/tiring.
I saw an advert/poster.
It was chilled/interesting/relaxing.
I went with my brother.
The final performance/entertainment/music ...

WRITING
Time phrases

On the day, I was ...
Just then, ...
After that, ...
After a while, ...
At the beginning, ...
Later on, ...
Eventually, ...

Connectors

I went to the park **and** we had a picnic.
My team played really well. **However**, they lost the match.
The weather was lovely in the morning, **but** it changed after lunch.
I was tired **so** I decided to go to bed.
We had to walk home **because** we missed the last bus.

127

LANGUAGE SUMMARY UNIT 2

GRAMMAR

Present perfect with *ever/never*

Questions
Have you/we/they **ever taken** a funny selfie?
Has he/she/it **ever travelled** around Europe?
Statements
I/You/We/They **have never flown** before.
He/She/It **has never seen** a shark.
Rules
We use the present perfect to talk about experiences in our lives when the exact time or date isn't important.
We often use it with *ever* and *never*. *Ever* means at some time in the past. We use *ever* in questions with the present perfect.
Never means at no time in the past. We use *never* in affirmative sentences.

Present perfect with *been/gone*

My dad**'s been** to New York. (He isn't in New York now.)
My dad**'s gone** to New York. (He's in New York now.)
Rules
We use *been* when we know that the person has returned from a journey.
We use *gone* when the person has not returned from a journey.

Present perfect with *just, already, yet*

Affirmative	Negative
I**'ve already unpacked** my bag.	I **haven't unpacked** my bag **yet**.
We**'ve already booked** our seats.	We **haven't booked** our seats **yet**.
You**'ve just had** lunch.	You **haven't had** lunch **yet**.
She**'s just arrived**.	She **hasn't arrived yet**.
Questions	Short answers
Have you **unpacked** your bag **yet**?	Yes, I **have**. / No, I **haven't**.
Has she **arrived yet**?	Yes, she **has**. / No, she **hasn't**.
Have they **finished** their homework **yet**?	Yes, they **have**. / No, they **haven't**.
Rules
We use *already* in affirmative sentences to talk about things that have happened sooner than we expected, or before a particular time.
We use *yet* in negative sentences and questions to talk about things that we expect to happen.
We use *just* for actions that happened a very short time ago.

VOCABULARY

Verbs for travel and holidays

arrive plan
book relax
depart return
explore set off
go abroad stay
pack unpack

Nouns for travel

announcement taxi rank
arrivals board the Underground
departures board ticket machine
information desk trolley
lost property office wheelie bag
queue
seat

SPEAKING

Asking for help and information

Which way is …?
Can you help us?
We're looking for …
Do you know where … is?
How far is …?
Can you show me … on this map?
It's just down … street.
It isn't far.
It's … minutes on foot.
It's that way.
It's a long way.

WRITING

Responding to news

It was great to hear from you.
Thanks for your message/news.
Have you … yet?
I'm having such a great time.
I've just arrived in …
Apart from that, …
That's all for now.
Hope to see you soon.

really, so, such

It's **really** cold!
These weeks are going **so** fast!
I'm having **such a** great time!
They sell **such** cool T-shirts.

LANGUAGE SUMMARY
UNIT 3

GRAMMAR

Present perfect with *How long ...?*, *for* and *since*

How long ...?	**How long have** you **known** Sophie? **How long have** they **lived** in London?
for	I**'ve been** here **for** three hours. We **haven't seen** him **for** two months.
since	He**'s worked** as a doctor **since** 2012. They **haven't eaten since** 7 o'clock.
since + past simple	He**'s worked** as a doctor **since** he **left** university.

Rules

We use *How long?* + the present perfect to ask questions about the duration of a situation.

We use *for* with a period of time, e.g. *for five years*, *for six weeks*, *for a long time*.

We use *since* with a fixed time in the past. We use it with times, dates, years and seasons, e.g. *since eleven o'clock*, *since 1 January*, *since 2005*, *since last summer*.

We use *since* + past simple in a present perfect sentence to describe when a situation started, e.g. *since I was ten years old*, *since we were at school together*.

Present perfect and past simple

Present perfect

I **'ve eaten** in that restaurant lots of times.
We **haven't been** to the new café in the shopping centre.

Past simple

I **had** dinner at an Italian restaurant on Saturday.
We **didn't go** to Sophie's party last night.

Questions

Have you **tried** the new Japanese restaurant?
Yes, we **have**. We **ate** there last weekend.
What **did** you **have**?
We **had** sushi. It **was** excellent!

Rules

We use the present perfect to talk about recent experiences or events in our lives, when what has happened is more important than the specific time it happened.

We use the past simple to talk about finished actions and situations, especially when we say when they happened.

We often use the present perfect to ask about recent experiences, but then we use the past simple to ask for and give more information.

VOCABULARY

Food and drink adjectives

creamy	frozen	sour
crispy	raw	spicy
crunchy	salty	sweet
fresh	savoury	

Cooking methods and menus

bake	microwave	ingredient
barbecue	roast	main course
boil	stir fry	side dish
fry	dessert	snack
grill	homemade	starter

SPEAKING

Expressing preferences

I would / I'd prefer ... (+ noun)
I would / I'd prefer to ... (+ verb)
I'd rather ... (+ verb + than ...)
I'd rather not ... (+ verb)
Would you rather ... (+ verb)?
Would you prefer ... (+ noun)?
Yes, I would. / No, I wouldn't.

WRITING

Describing a meal

I decided to try ...
My starter/dessert was ...
This (rice) dish contains ...
For the main course I had a Turkish/Spanish/Mexican dish called ...
In my opinion, it was delicious/amazing/the best meal I've ever had.
It was disappointing/terrible/the worst meal I've ever had.

Order of adjectives

You can use two adjectives together to make your writing more interesting.
Adjectives usually follow this order:

opinion	size/shape/colour	nationality/type
tasty	small	traditional
spicy	large	Japanese
delicious	round	vegetarian
plain	colourful	Mexican
disgusting		

LANGUAGE SUMMARY
UNIT 4

GRAMMAR
Future forms

be going to and will
Affirmative
Their company **is going to be** a great success.
We **will** probably **have** a better life in the USA.
I **don't think** Rafael Nadal **will** win the match.
Negative
Look at the sky. It **isn't going to rain** today.
Robots definitely **won't do** my job in the future.
Questions
Are you **going to get** a job this summer?
Will Brazil **win** the World Cup next year?
Rules

We use *be going to* for future intentions and predictions based on information or evidence.

We use *will* for general predictions about the future.

We often use *will* with the adverbs *possibly*, *probably* and *definitely* to express degrees of certainty. The adverb goes after *will*, but before *won't*.

We often use *will* after the phrases *I think* and *I don't think*.

Future continuous	
+	They**'ll be waiting** for you when your plane arrives.
−	She **won't be working** during the summer holiday.
?	**Will** you **be serving** customers in your new job?
Rules	

We use the future continuous for actions that will be in progress at a particular time in the future.

First conditional: *if* and *unless*; *might* vs *will* + adverbs

Situation	Result
if/unless + present simple	*will/won't* + infinitive
If she **works** hard,	she **will pass** her exams.
Unless she **works** hard,	she **won't pass** her exams.
If she **goes** to university,	she **will probably get** a better job.
If he **moves** to London,	he **might get** a better job.
Rules	

We use the first conditional with *if* and *unless* to talk about possible future events and their consequences. We use *unless* to mean *if not*.

We use the present simple for the situation (the *if* clause) and *will* or *won't* + infinitive for the result (the main clause).

We use the adverbs *possibly* and *probably* or the modal verb *might* when the consequences are not certain.

When the situation (the *if* clause) is first, we use a comma after it. When the result comes first, there is no comma.

VOCABULARY
Jobs and job sectors

agriculture and environment
banking
care worker
catering
construction
education
healthcare
IT
law

leisure and tourism
media
music tutor
retail, sales and customer service
sports instructor
tour guide
web designer
wildlife photographer

Adjectives of personality

brave
calm
confident
creative
curious
honest

independent
patient
positive
sensible
shy
sociable

SPEAKING
Giving opinions

I'm (not) sure.
I'm quite keen on the idea because …
I reckon …
That's why …
I'm (not) sure you're right.
To be honest …
That's the reason …
I (also) think …

WRITING
Speculating about the future

I often wonder what …
I guess …
I suppose …
I hope to / I hope I'll/we'll …

Future time expressions

Next year, …
After my exams, …
In five/ten years' time, …
One day, …
When I'm eighteen/older, …
In the future, …

LANGUAGE SUMMARY
UNIT 5

GRAMMAR
Second conditional

Situation	Result
If Adam **was** taller,	he **would be** very good at basketball.
If I **won** the lottery,	I**'d buy** a Ferrari.
If there **were** fewer cars on the road,	the air **would be** cleaner.
If I **were** you,	I **would apologize** to your teacher.

Rules

We use the second conditional to talk about unreal or unlikely events and their consequences.

We use *if* + past simple for the situation and *would/wouldn't* + infinitive for the result.

We can start the sentence with either the situation (*If* …) or the result. When the situation is first, we use a comma after it. When the result comes first, there is no comma.

We also use the second conditional to give advice with *If I were you, …*.

Obligation: *must*; Necessity: *need to / have to*

Obligation: *must / mustn't* + infinitive

We **must wear** our uniforms when we're at school.
We **mustn't use** our mobile phones during the lessons.

Necessity: *need to / don't need to* (+ infinitive); *have to / don't have to* (+ infinitive)

I **need to finish** my Maths homework this afternoon.
It's Sunday tomorrow so you **don't need to get up** early.
I **have to get up** at six o'clock on school days.
You **don't have to drive** me to the station. I can walk.

Rules

We use the modal verb *must* when it's important to do something. We use *mustn't* when it's important NOT to do something.

We use *need to* and *have to* to talk about things that are necessary. We use *don't need to* and *don't have to* to talk about things that are not necessary.

The past simple of *have to* and *must* is *had to* and the past simple of *don't have to* is *didn't have to*.

Advice: *should / ought to*

Advice: *should/shouldn't* (+ infinitive); *ought to/oughtn't to* (+ infinitive)

You **should/shouldn't help** your sister with her homework.
You **ought to buy** your grandma a birthday present.
You **oughtn't to drink** coffee in the evening.

Rules

We often use the modal verbs *should* and *shouldn't* to give advice.

Ought to and *oughtn't to* have similar meanings to *should* and *shouldn't*, but are less common.

VOCABULARY
Communication verbs

apologize	interrupt
argue	repeat
complain	scream
discuss	shout
explain	translate
gossip	whisper

Communication nouns

communication	interruption
definition	pronunciation
description	punctuation
discussion	repetition
explanation	suggestion
expression	translation

SPEAKING
Asking for and giving clarification

Can you explain?
What do/did you mean?
Sorry, I didn't catch that.
Can you repeat that?
Could you say that again?
What was that?
I'm not sure I understand.
I meant that …
I said that …
I didn't mean that, I meant …
I can explain.

WRITING
Giving reasons

(just) because
as
because of (+ noun phrase)
due to (+ noun phrase)
that's why …
the reason is that …

Talking about purpose

I need to revise **in order to** pass my exam.
He has to revise **so that** he can pass his exam.

LANGUAGE SUMMARY UNIT 6

GRAMMAR

Relative pronouns

Relative pronouns

The people **who/that** come to this gym are mainly quite young.
The tennis racket **which/that** you gave me is broken.
That's the pool **where** Imogen and I go swimming.

Rules

We use the relative pronouns *who/that*, *which/that* or *where* to make it clear which people, thing(s) or place(s) we are talking about.

Indefinite pronouns

I'd like to learn **something** about the game.
Nobody can run faster than him.
There are football supporters **everywhere**.
Somebody was calling his name.

Rules

We use indefinite pronouns to refer to people, things or places without saying exactly who or what they are.

Ability: *can, could, be able to*

Now I **can understand** English films.
We **couldn't hear** what she was saying.
She **wasn't able to come** to my birthday party.
I'**ll be able to drive** you to the station tomorrow morning.

Rules

We use the modal *can/can't* + infinitive to talk about present ability.
We use the modal *could/couldn't* + infinitive to talk about past ability.
We use *be able to* + infinitive to talk about present, past or future ability. We often use it when talking about specific events.

Permission: *can/can't, be allowed to*

Can I **borrow** your pen, please?
You **can use** my phone to call your mum.
You **can't take** photos in the museum.
You **aren't allowed to use** your mobile phone in the exams.
Are we **allowed to wear** our shoes in the gym?

Rules

We use the modal *can/can't* (+ infinitive) to ask for, give or refuse permission.
We use *be allowed to* or *can/can't* (+ infinitive) to talk about things we have (or don't have) permission to do.

VOCABULARY

Sports verbs

attack
attend
beat
catch
compete
defend

hit
organize
score
support
throw
train

Adverbs of manner

angrily
badly
brilliantly
calmly
carefully
carelessly

confidently
energetically
lazily
nervously
terribly
well

SPEAKING

Giving a group presentation

I'd like to introduce …
We're here to present …
I'm going to hand over to (name) who …
First of all,
To start with, …
(Jamie) will explain (the details/rules).
We hope you like …
Thank you for listening.
Are there any questions?
Thank you for your time.

WRITING

Using questions as headings

Where is it?
What are your opening hours?
Is it expensive?
Can I have a party there?
Can we bring our own food and drink?

Making adjectives stronger or weaker

The food was**n't very** tasty.
The restaurant was **quite** expensive.
The match was **very** exciting.
That horror film was **really** scary!
When I got home I was **extremely** tired.

LANGUAGE SUMMARY
UNIT 7

GRAMMAR
Present simple passive

Affirmative	Negative
The plant **is used** to treat headaches.	This animal **isn't** usually **seen** in Scotland.
Sadly, these animals **are** still **kept** as pets.	Olives **aren't grown** by farmers in the UK.
Questions	**Short answers**
Is the insect **found** in this region?	Yes, it **is**. / No, it **isn't**.
Are lots of people **attacked** by sharks?	Yes, they **are**. / No, they **aren't**.

Rules

We form the present simple passive with the present simple of be (*am*, *is*, *are*) and the past participle.

We usually add *by* when we say who or what does the action.

We use the passive when the person or thing doing the action isn't important or we don't know who is doing it.

We often use the passive to describe processes.

Past simple passive

Affirmative	Negative
The plant **was discovered** in 1892.	This **wasn't understood** at the time.
Many whales **were killed** during this period.	The animals **weren't given** enough food.
Questions	**Short answers**
Was the forest completely **destroyed**?	Yes, it **was**. / No, it **wasn't**.
Were the bones **found** near here?	Yes, they **were**. / No, they **weren't**.

Rules

We form the past simple passive with the past simple of be (*was*, *were*) and the past participle.

VOCABULARY
The natural environment

cave	sand
cliff	sunlight
coast	sunrise
glacier	sunset
ice	valley
rock	wave

Environment verbs

clean up	recycle
collect	reuse
destroy	save
poison	throw away
pollute	waste
protect	

SPEAKING
Agreeing and disagreeing

Yes, I agree (with you/that).
That's true, but …
(Perhaps) you're right.
I (totally) agree.
That's a good point.
I think that's a great idea.
Absolutely!
You're (definitely) right about that!
Sorry, I don't agree.
I don't think that's true.
I'm not sure I agree with (you/that).

WRITING
Arguing for and against

We regularly hear news stories about …
News stories regularly tell us that …
Although many believe …, there are also …
On the one hand, …
On the other hand, …
In conclusion,
To conclude, I agree/disagree …

Giving more information

My sister **also** enjoys playing video games.
as well as …
In addition to that, …
My cousin came to the concert, **too**.
What's more, …

LANGUAGE SUMMARY UNIT 8

GRAMMAR

Past perfect simple

Affirmative	Negative
When I arrived at school, the exam **had** already **started**.	I failed my Maths exam because I **hadn't revised** properly.
When we **had finished** our homework, we watched a film.	After he **had finished** his exams, he had a party.
Questions	**Short answers**
Had you **flown** before your trip to London?	Yes, I **had**. / No, I **hadn't**.
Had Jack **left** the party before you got there?	Yes, he **had**. / No, he **hadn't**.

Rules

We form the past perfect with *had* + past participle.

We use the past perfect to talk about an action that happened before another action in the past.

We often use the past perfect and the past simple in the same sentence. We use the past simple for the main action. We use the past perfect for the action that occurred at an earlier time.

We often use *already*, *after*, *before* and *when* in sentences with the past perfect.

Modals of possibility and certainty

Apps **can** be good for learning languages.
This website **could** be really useful for our project.
Be careful! That dog **might** be dangerous.
We **may** have a new English teacher next term.
That **can't** be Joe! He's on holiday this week.
He **must** be rich. He's got three houses!

Rules

We use *can* when something is generally possible.

We use *could/might/may* + infinitive to talk about things that are possible in the present and the future.

We use *can't* to say that something is not possible.

We use *must*, *might*, *may* and *could* to speculate about the present and future.

We use *must* when we are certain that something is true.

We use *might*, *may* and *could* when we are not sure.

VOCABULARY

Education words

achievement
attention
challenge
curriculum
fail
memory
pass

progress
report
result
revision
skill
timetable
topic

Phrasal verbs

carry on
hand out
join in
look around
look up
pick up

put away
show off
stay behind
tidy up
turn up

SPEAKING

Asking for news and reacting

What have you been up to?
Have I missed anything?
Did you have a good weekend?
Apparently, …
It says … here / on the website.
Have you heard about …?
Did you know (that / about) …?
That's (+ adjective).
No way! / What happened?
Really? / You're joking!
I didn't (even) know …

WRITING

Using informal language

Has a teacher ever surprised you?
Guess what?
Have you got any teacher stories to share?
Let me tell you about …
I'd love to hear all about …
Well, this morning …
Next, …
It turns out (that) …

Exclamatory phrases

Amazing!
How exciting!
What a cool (teacher)!
I couldn't believe it!
I'd love to (hear them / see it)!

LANGUAGE SUMMARY
UNIT 9

GRAMMAR
Reported speech

Direct speech	Reported speech
Present simple	**Past simple**
Tom and Joe: We **want** musicians to perform here.	They said (that) they **wanted** musicians to perform there.
Present continuous	**Past continuous**
Sarah: I**'m looking** for a dress to wear to my cousin's wedding.	Sarah said (that) she **was looking** for a dress to wear to her cousin's wedding.
Present perfect	**Past perfect**
Tom: We**'ve** always **bought** our fruit and vegetables from this market.	Tom said (that) they**'d** always **bought** their fruit and vegetables from that market.
Past simple	**Past perfect**
Sophie: I **didn't go** to the market on Saturday.	Sophie told me (that) she **hadn't been** to the market on Saturday.
Rules	

When we report what someone said in the past (*said/told*), the tense of the verb changes.

Be careful! Pronouns and possessive adjectives also need to change.

We use a present tense reporting verb (e.g. *say/tell*) (+ person) to report present statements that are generally true.

Martha's mum: I **enjoy** going shopping.

Martha: My mum **says** she **enjoys** going shopping.

Reported questions

Yes/No questions	
Direct speech	Reported speech
Maria: **Do** you **want** a drink?	She asked me **if** I **wanted** a drink.
Ethan: **Are** you **going to** stay?	Ethan asked **whether** we **were going to** stay.
Wh- questions	
Direct speech	Reported speech
Amy and Mia: **Why have** you **started** going to the gym?	They asked me **why** I **had started** going to the gym.
Anna: **How did** you **get** here?	She asked me **how** I **had got** there.
Thomas: **Where are** you **meeting**?	Thomas asked us **where** we **were meeting**.
Rules	

To report a *Yes/No* question, we use a past tense reporting verb (e.g. *asked*) (+ person) + *if* or *whether* …

To report a *Wh-* question, we use a past tense reporting verb (e.g. *asked*) (+ person) + *who/what/when/where/why/how* …

Be careful! Pronouns and possessive adjectives also need to change.

The tense changes are the same as for reported statements and we don't use *do* or *did*.

VOCABULARY
Shopping nouns

assistant	payment
chain	product
checkout	purchase
customer	receipt
delivery	refund
offer	service

Adjectives and affixes

colourful	reliable
comfortable	successful
fashionable	suitable
helpful	useful
powerful	valuable
reasonable	wonderful

SPEAKING
Persuading

Are you sure you …?
It would be really helpful if …
Go on, it'll be …
Why don't you …?
I'm sure you could …
Honestly, I think you'll enjoy it.
Please say you'll …
You won't regret it.
You'll have a great time.

WRITING
Writing a review

My favourite shop is …
The best thing about it is …
I (also) find … really helpful/useful.
The worst thing is …
The main disadvantage is that …
To sum up, I would say …

Recommending

I would/wouldn't recommend it.
It's really worth a visit.
You'll love it!
You really won't be disappointed!

135

IRREGULAR VERBS LIST

Infinitive		Past simple		Past participle	
beat	/biːt/	beat	/biːt/	beaten	/ˈbiːtn/
begin	/bɪˈgɪn/	began	/bɪˈgæn/	begun	/bɪˈgʌn/
break	/breɪk/	broke	/brəʊk/	broken	/ˈbrəʊkən/
bring	/brɪŋ/	brought	/brɔːt/	brought	/brɔːt/
build	/bɪld/	built	/bɪlt/	built	/bɪlt/
catch	/kætʃ/	caught	/kɔːt/	caught	/kɔːt/
choose	/tʃuːz/	chose	/tʃəʊz/	chosen	/ˈtʃəʊzn/
come	/kʌm/	came	/keɪm/	come	/kʌm/
cost	/kɒst/	cost	/kɒst/	cost	/kɒst/
draw	/drɔː/	drew	/druː/	drawn	/drɔːn/
drive	/draɪv/	drove	/drəʊv/	driven	/ˈdrɪvn/
fall	/fɔːl/	fell	/fel/	fallen	/ˈfɔːlən/
feel	/fiːl/	felt	/felt/	felt	/felt/
find	/faɪnd/	found	/faʊnd/	found	/faʊnd/
fly	/flaɪ/	flew	/fluː/	flown	/fləʊn/
forget	/fəˈget/	forgot	/fəˈgɒt/	forgotten	/fəˈgɒtn/
get	/get/	got	/gɒt/	got	/gɒt/
give	/gɪv/	gave	/geɪv/	given	/ˈgɪvn/
go	/gəʊ/	went	/went/	gone/been	/gɒn, biːn/
grow	/grəʊ/	grew	/gruː/	grown	/grəʊn/
hear	/hɪə(r)/	heard	/hɜːd/	heard	/hɜːd/
keep	/kiːp/	kept	/kept/	kept	/kept/
know	/nəʊ/	knew	/njuː/	known	/nəʊn/
leave	/liːv/	left	/left/	left	/left/
lose	/luːz/	lost	/lɒst/	lost	/lɒst/
meet	/miːt/	met	/met/	met	/met/
pay	/peɪ/	paid	/peɪd/	paid	/peɪd/
put	/pʊt/	put	/pʊt/	put	/pʊt/
read	/riːd/	read	/red/	read	/red/
ride	/raɪd/	rode	/rəʊd/	ridden	/ˈrɪdn/
ring	/rɪŋ/	rang	/ræŋ/	rung	/rʌŋ/
run	/rʌn/	ran	/ræn/	run	/rʌn/
say	/seɪ/	said	/sed/	said	/sed/
see	/siː/	saw	/sɔː/	seen	/siːn/
sell	/sel/	sold	/səʊld/	sold	/səʊld/
send	/send/	sent	/sent/	sent	/sent/
sing	/sɪŋ/	sang	/sæŋ/	sung	/sʌŋ/
sit	/sɪt/	sat	/sæt/	sat	/sæt/
sleep	/sliːp/	slept	/slept/	slept	/slept/
speak	/spiːk/	spoke	/spəʊk/	spoken	/ˈspəʊkən/
spend	/spend/	spent	/spent/	spent	/spent/
stand	/stænd/	stood	/stʊd/	stood	/stʊd/
swim	/swɪm/	swam	/swæm/	swum	/swʌm/
take	/teɪk/	took	/tʊk/	taken	/ˈteɪkən/
teach	/tiːtʃ/	taught	/tɔːt/	taught	/tɔːt/
tell	/tel/	told	/təʊld/	told	/təʊld/
think	/θɪŋk/	thought	/θɔːt/	thought	/θɔːt/
throw	/θrəʊ/	threw	/θruː/	thrown	/θrəʊn/
wake	/weɪk/	woke	/wəʊk/	woken	/ˈwəʊkən/
wear	/weə(r)/	wore	/wɔː(r)/	worn	/wɔːn/
win	/wɪn/	won	/wʌn/	won	/wʌn/
write	/raɪt/	wrote	/rəʊt/	written	/ˈrɪtn/